Radical Islam ~~At the Door~~
In The House

The Plan to Take America
For the Global Islamic State

Michael Coffman, Ph.D. and Kate Mathieson
©2013

Published by Environmental Perspectives, Inc.
Bangor, Maine

Radical Islam ~~At the Door~~ In The House

The Plan to Take America For The Global Islamic State

Michael Coffman, Ph.D. and Kate Mathieson
© 2013

Printed in the United States of America. No part of this publication may be reproduced or transmitted in any form or by any means, mechanical or electronic, including photocopying and recording, or by any information storage and retrieval system, without permission in writing from author (except by a reviewer, who may quote brief passages and/or show brief video clips in a review).

Disclaimer: The publisher and the authors make no representations or warranties with respect to the accuracy or completeness of the contents of this work and specifically disclaim all warranties, including without limitation warranties of fitness for a particular purpose. No warranty may be created or extended by sales or promotional materials. The advice and strategies contained herein may not be suitable for every situation. Neither the publisher nor the author shall be liable for damages arising therefrom. The fact that an organization or website is referred to in this work as a citation and/or a potential source of further information does not mean that the author or the publisher endorses the information the organization or website may provide or recommendations it may make. Further, readers should be aware that internet websites listed in this work may have changed or disappeared between when this work was written and when it is read.

Cover: The White House (public domain) and the Crescent Moon and Star of Islam

ISBN-13: 978-1481822602
ISBN-10: 1481822608

BISAC: Religion/Political Science/Political Ideologies

Environmental Perspectives, Inc. Publishing
6 Heather Rd.
Bangor, Maine 04401

Contents

Radical Islam ~~At the Door~~ In the House ii
Contents iii
Preface v
1 - Islamization 1
    Two Major Islamic Sects 2
        Shi'ite 2
        Sunni 4
    Shari'a Law 6
2 - Civilization Jihad 9
    The Muslim Brotherhood 9
        The Brotherhood Strategy 11
        Phases of the World Underground Movement Plan 13
        Ongoing Efforts 14
    Obama Supporting Islamist Activity 19
3 - Wahhabi Islam: The Royal Puppet Masters 21
    Saudi Arabia—Birthplace of Wahhabism 22
    9/11 Inconsistencies 25
4 – Islamic Networking to Penetrate and Influence 29
    Islamists in Key Positions of Power 31
        Huma and Saleha Abedin 31
        Dr. Abdullah Nasif 35
        Mohamed Elibiary 35
        Mohamed Magid 37
    Of Corruption, Deception and Outright Evil 38
        Education 41
    Attack and Destroy 43

5 - The Obama Connection 45
    The Inexplicable Explained? 46
    The Islamist Obamas in Kenya 51
    Obama's Fundamental Transformation of America 54
6 – Real-World Biblical Implications 57
    The Mahdi vs. Jesus 59
        The Mahdi 59
        Jesus 62
    The Greatest of All Deceivers 66
7 – Jihad and the God of War 71
    The Destroyer 71
        Salvation and Jihad 73
        Jihad, the Bible and the "Mark" 76
    The Treaty of Hudaibiyah 79
    The Great Delusion 82
    Islamists and Progressive Liberals Linked? 82

Preface

The information in this book has been the most difficult we have ever written. I (Kate) have wrestled fears I didn't even know I had. I have come face to face with my own bigotry and anger. When I began researching to write this book, with 9/11 still very fresh in my memory, I really didn't care if Muslims were killing each other in foreign countries. I didn't care that they were dying. It's not that I wished them ill, or wanted them to die, or suffer. I simply didn't care. I was still so angry about the losses we have suffered at the hands of the Islamic Jihadist terrorists, that I found it very difficult in my heart to care if they faced tragedy.

We are very grateful that this book took so long to write. In the intervening months, we (Kate more than Mike) have been buried in the lives of Muslims from countries around the world. While no person can truly know what another thinks or feels, we believe we have a much better understanding of how the Jihadist Muslims have come to be the way that they are.

We are no longer angry at them, but rather, we are angry at the deceiver who holds them by the throat with a death grip that only Jesus the Messiah can loose. Many of you who read to this point will put the book down in disgust because we deal with "religion." Well, guess what? Islam *is* a religion as well as a form of government that seeks to dominate you, and failing that, to destroy you. You'd better understand what is happening.

We have come to the place where we long for each and every person, including Muslims, to know true freedom. We are not talking political freedom, though we want them to have that; we are not talking religious freedom; though we wish they could experience that as well. We are talking about the kind of freedom that comes in knowing that the God who created you would never require *your* blood to save you.

The God who created all of us required blood, yes. But in His love and great mercy, and by His plan, laid before the foundation of the world, He sent His own Son to be the bloody sacrifice for all of us sinners. And surely that is what we are. Our death can never atone for our individual sin. No Muslim's death can atone for his either; no matter what the Qur'an, Hadith and other writings promise. That is the deception. Muslims believe it is an abomination to say their deity could ever have a son. But God did have a Son. The God of Abraham, Isaac and Jacob, is also the God of three other Jewish boys; Peter, James and John. They all believed in the Son of God. The first three in the Promise, the latter three in the Promise fulfilled.

The deity of the Qur'an requires allegiance at the point of a sword. The God of the Bible is a God of freedom. He allows us to choose to come to Him. He will never force, nor does he ask his followers to use force on those around them. Our prayer is that all will come to the foot of the cross and allow the God who made them to give them the only true freedom.

We are pleased to learn that the Muslim world is experiencing a revival with an estimated 16,000 a day coming to Jesus as he shows them Himself and His love. Stories coming out of the Middle-East can only be described as miraculous in nature as new believers in Jesus describe "road to Damascus" type experiences, where Jesus is literally visiting them in dreams and visions.

In the first chapter of the book of Jeremiah, God tells Jeremiah to look at the almond tree and to remember that He is always watching. He used the almond tree because the two Hebrew words for almond and watching sound very similar. They are almost homonyms. God wanted Jeremiah to know that He was *always* watching and keeping an account of what was happening, especially when things are at their worst. God was telling Jeremiah this at the time when Israel was taken into captivity. With the constant reminder of the almond tree, God helped Jeremiah to remember the He *always* does what he says he will do. People often ask, "how can a loving God allow bad things to happen?" He is keeping an account. There will be a reckoning. That is a certainty.

Evil is permeating America like never before. The penetration of our society by Islam is but one of the attacks on this great nation.

Volumes have been written on the subject, but few Americans have read them. By condensing the information we hope you will begin to understand the danger. We also hope you don't put this book down because we deal, in part with "religion." Neither of us like melodrama. But, it is critical you understand what is happening. Your life, and the lives of your children for generations to come, depend on what you do once you have this information.

1 - Islamization

"The American mediocre mind is no match to 14 centuries of Islamic deception..."
Walid Shoebat, former Islamic Terrorist

Many say America was blindsided by 9/11. It is true that the masses were blindsided. However, for those who took the time to listen, it was blatantly clear something was coming. It was reported in the August, 1999 issue of *Discerning the Times*, (a publication of EPI) "The likelihood of a terrorist attack within the borders of the continental U.S. seems to be more a question of when, rather than if, it will occur."[1] That article stated that the likely perpetrator of the terror would be Osama Bin Laden.

The author was not psychic. She was a small time journalist living in a very rural community with nothing but the fledgling '90's internet at her disposal. She certainly didn't have any kind of security clearance. How did she know something was coming? Simple, she listened to what the Islamic radicals were saying. They were publicly proclaiming and threatening America. And that journalist, quite simply, believed what they said. Not all Muslims want the war they are waging here, but for all who are old enough to remember 9/11, it is very clear just exactly what those who want an Islamic caliphate are willing to do to get it.

We must listen to what they are saying all the more now. When they say they want to destroy the West, they really mean it. These men are not fringe hacks. They are KEY political and government leaders within the global Islamic movement. In 1991, the Muslim Brotherhood developed their "Explanatory Memorandum on the General Strategic Goals of the Group." This document claimed, "A kind of grand Jihad in eliminating and destroying the Western civilization from within, sabotaging its miserable house with their own hands and the hands of the believers so that it is eliminated and god's religion is made victorious over all other religions." This statement very succinctly states what they want to do. Why does our government keep ignoring it?

Two Major Islamic Sects

Just like other major religions, there are numerous sects of Islam. Although others will be discussed later, two dominate Islam and are the source of much conflict. They are Shia and Sunni. Both sects believe that fundamental Islam and Shari'a Law must dominate and govern the entire world in a global caliphate. Both believe in an Islamic savior called the Mahdi who will appear and wage war with all non-Islamic nations to establish the global caliphate.

Shi'ite

The Shi'ite sect of Islam goes one step further than the Sunni sect. Followers of Shia Islam believe that at the end of all things, there will be chaos and global war that will usher in the 12th Imam. The Shi'ites believe that the 12th Imam who lived in the 9th century, Muḥammad ibn al-Ḥasan al-Mahdi, did not die, but rather was hidden away by their god and will return in the end days. Called the Mahdi (who is a Muslim cleric anointed by their god to lead); he will kill everyone who doesn't adhere to this very radical form of Islam. Then he will set up his global government. They further believe there MUST be great global chaos for their Mahdi to show up. It is sobering to know that 670 million Muslims expect the Mahdi in their lifetime.[2]

Iran's supreme leader, Ayatollah Ali Khamenei, has said, "The issue of Imam Mahdi is of utmost importance, and his reappearance has been clearly stated in our holy [Shi'ite] religion of Islam. We must study and remind ourselves of the end of times and Imam Mahdi's era. …We must prepare the environment for the coming so that the great leader will come." In other words, their belief system demands that creating global chaos, especially war with Israel, is the only way to have the Mahdi return. So when the SUPREME leader of Iran says he needs to prepare the requisite environment for the Mahdi to come, it is crystal clear what Khamenei means; he *wants* war.

Mahmoud Ahmadinejad, the current Iranian president, agrees. That name is one that most Americans know by now, though it is doubtful they can spell it. Ahmadinejad really made himself known to most Americans, even by people outside of politics, when he publically called for the annihilation of the Nation of Israel in 2005, and the press ran with it.[3]

The Iranian leader repeatedly rants against Israel and the United States. In his speech before the UN in 2011, he incessantly railed against the United States[4] so maliciously that many diplomats got up and walked out on him. In that speech he accused the United States of starting WWI &WWII; of provoking and encouraging Saddam Hussein to invade Iran; and he called for the world to collectively come under the leadership of the Islamic Mahdi. Ahmadinejad has declared that:

> "This movement is certainly on its rightful path of creation, ensuring a promising future for humanity. A future that will be built when humanity initiates to trend [sic] the path of the divine prophets and the righteous under the leadership of Imam al-Mahdi..."[5]

On his blog in February of 2012, Ahmadinejad said that *this year* was "beginning of the imamate of the Imam Al-Mahdi." Whichever term they use, "New Order," "imamate", "caliphate", they all mean one thing: A world-wide government under Islam.[6] His proclamation takes a sinister meaning when Ahmadinejad clearly believed Iran would have a nuclear weapon by the end of 2012 or 2013. According to the International Atomic Energy Agency, during the last year alone, Iran has doubled the number of centrifuges in its underground nuclear facility in Qom.[7] Iran is indeed on track to have its first nuclear bomb by 2013.

In his speech before the UN in 2012, Ahmadinejad was even more public about his focus on the imminent coming of his Mahdi— his choice for a world leader. He used a lot of nice sounding words like "freedom", and "justice" and "kindness" in his 2012 speech before the UN, but those words clearly don't mean to him what they mean to westerners. His freedom means freedom *from* the laws of man and adherence *to* the laws of Shari'a. Justice means justice according to Shari'a. (More on Shari'a later)

Extreme Sunni and Shi'ite followers of Islam may disagree about how the Mahdi will come and who he will be, but they are in total agreement he will come and usher in their global Islamic caliphate and the destruction of Israel.

Ahmadinejad trumpets freedom and justice while calling for the destruction of the "Zionists (Israel) AND the United states."[8] It is shocking, and more than a little disconcerting that a Holocaust denying national leader with such openly murderous, anti-Semitic, hatred is invited to speak at the UN.[9]

Even as Ahmadinejad is claiming that his Mahdi will want love, peace and dancing through the daisies for everyone, the Iranian Defense Minister, Ahmad Vahidi, has publicly stated that Iran is ready to go to war because they believe they are in the era of "The Coming."[10] Vahidi is on Interpol's most wanted list for his involvement in the slaughter of 85 people in Buenos Aires in 1994 when a Jewish Community Center was bombed.

Sunni

Although the Sunni sect of Islam does not believe the 12th Imam is the Mahdi, their beliefs are no less severe than those of the Shi'ites. Grand Mufti Sheik Abdul Aziz bin Abdullah, the primary religious leader for the Arabian Peninsula, makes far reaching decisions in both the religious and legal realms. A delegation from Kuwait had come to him because they wanted to pass legislation that would prevent the building of Christian churches. His ruling was that there were not to be two religions on the Arabian Peninsula and that it is, "necessary to destroy all the [Christian] churches of the region."[11]

As it is, there is not freedom of religion in many of the countries that are Muslim today. Non-Muslims in Saudi Arabia have to worship in secret and are always at risk of being found out by the mutawa, or morality police, which could lead to arrest and legal ramifications. Christians all over the Muslim world face persecution, imprisonment and even death.

Sunni Cleric, Sheik Yusuf al-Qaradawi was banished from Egypt as well as the US and Israel for his support of violence against soldiers from these countries. He is a key spiritual advisor to the Muslim Brotherhood. Al-Qaradawi was brought back to Egypt with great fanfare in 2011 after years of exile. Upon his return, he gave his first public message in Egypt in decades. At this event in Tahrir square, he had the crowd of over 2 million people loudly chanting over and over again, "martyrs in the millions we march to Jerusalem." *The New York Times* article about the speech made the whole thing sound like something worth celebrating.[12] In reality it was a murderous rant calling for the utter destruction of Israel.[13]

In order to understand where the radical Muslims at work here in the United States want to take this nation, we need only look to Egypt. Their modus operandi is to build a solid but hidden governing framework which is ready to be moved into place once they cause chaos. That is exactly what happened in Egypt. Democracy was used to disguise a terrorist as a diplomat. While many in the West were heralding the "Arabic Spring," those with eyes to see and ears to hear knew that an Islamic winter was soon to come.

During the Egyptian presidential elections a leading Muslim cleric, Imam Safwat Hijazi, gave a speech in support of then Muslim Brotherhood candidate Muhammad Morsi. Hijazi proclaimed,

"We can see how the dream of the Islamic caliphate is being realized, Allah willing, by Dr. Muhammad Morsi, and his brothers, his supporters, and his political party. We can see how the great dream, shared by us all... the United States of the Arabs will be restored, Allah willing... by this man and his supporters. The capital of the caliphate will be Jerusalem. Our capital will not be Cairo, Mecca or Medina. It shall be Jerusalem."

Hijazi then led the crowd in a call and answer chant where he called out, "Morsi will liberate Gaza tomorrow." The response was, "I am an Egyptian and proud of it!" They ended chanting loudly, and in unison, "Allahu akbar," which means "Allah is greater." Then he said, echoing Sheik Yusuf al-Qaradawi from a year earlier, "Our cry shall be, martyrs march toward Jerusalem." The huge crowd then sang a song together over and over, complete with band, "Come on, you lovers of martyrdom, you are all Hamas. Banish the sleep from the eyes of all Jews. Forget about the whole world. Brandish your weapons. Say your prayers. Brandish your weapons and pray to the lord."

Imam Safwat Hijazi went on, "I say… from the heart of Egypt so that the whole world may hear. We say it loud and clear. Jerusalem is our goal. We shall pray in Jerusalem or else we shall all die as martyrs on its threshold. Millions of martyrs march toward Jerusalem."

This was a *campaign* speech. Morsi won that election. Morsi is a key leader within the Muslim Brotherhood.

Almost as soon as Morsi took office, he ordered the retirement of the powerful head of the country's armed forces, Field Marshal Mohammad Hussein Tantawi, and he cancelled a constitutional declaration aimed at curbing presidential powers. On November 22, 2012 Morsi even declared himself above the Egyptian Constitution and immune from any court.[14]

Although Morsi claims publically that he is not looking for an Islamic state, when he is in a setting away from the Western media he tells the truth. Before a group of college students in Cairo during an election speech in May, 2012, he proclaimed unashamedly, Egypt's Constitution should be based on the Qur'an and Shari'a law.

It is imperative to LISTEN to what these leaders are saying. Our nation's future depends on it. In that same speech Morsi said, "The Qur'an is our constitution, the Prophet is our leader, Jihad is our path and death in the name of Allah is our goal," Morsi went on to say that, today, Egypt is close as never before to the triumph of Islam at all the state levels. He further stated, "Today we can establish Shari'a law because our nation will acquire well-being only with Islam and Shari'a. The Muslim Brothers and the Freedom and Justice Party will be the conductors of these goals."[15] As expected, when the people voted on the Constitution, turnout was low because of intimidation. As forecast, it is based in Shari'a law.

Shari'a Law

Shari'a is the goal of this global movement. We see the Middle East on fire as government after government is toppled in favor of a Shari'a compliant government. Shari'a is not just a religious code. It is a constitution as well. Shari'a means "the path" in Arabic. It is their tool for totalitarian control. Many Muslims do not follow this path and are persecuted by other Muslims because of it.

Shari'a was developed over several hundred years. The sacred writings of Islam, the Qur'an and the Sunnah, the Hadith and the Sira, are interpreted and implemented through the caliphs, or leaders who issue fatwas, or judgments. It is also interpreted and implemented by scholarly works by influential academic institutions.

Shari'a is much more than a legal code. Shari'a precludes man-made laws, representative government, religious freedom, free speech, gender equality, and equality of Muslim and non-Muslim.

The treatment of women in Shari'a can be horrific. Shari'a puts men in absolute control of women. It is justified because proponents insist men know what is best for women. Shari'a calls for the automatic death of homosexuals; mandates Jihad, or holy war; mandates zakat, which includes supporting jihad financially; female genital mutilation and honor killings. This is the short list. Shari'a is already here in the United States. American judges have deferred to Shari'a in cases before them in 27 states in blatant violation of the U.S. Constitution. [16]

The Arab Spring is nothing but an effort to establish a caliphate. The Muslim Brotherhood is pushing Shari'a the hardest and most aggressively. They use whatever means necessary, including deception, or taqiyya, which is obligatory lying for the faith, to achieve their goals.[17] It's nothing more than situational ethics. They live here among us to learn how we think, and how to overcome us.

Morsi himself came to the U.S. to get his Ph.D. He taught college here for three years at California State University, Northridge. He understands the western mind far better than we can understand what makes him tick. They have infiltrated our country at every level; our educational institutions, our legal system, our government.

The Muslim Brotherhood was founded by Hassan Al Banna who said, "it is the nature of Islam to dominate, not to be dominated; to impose its laws on all nations and to extend its power to the entire planet."[18] In 1998, they were one of several Muslim organizations calling themselves "The Global Front." This group declared war against "Jews and the people of the cross." The Brotherhood's creed:

"Allah is our objective. The prophet is our leader. The Qur'an is our law. Jihad is our way. Dying in the way of Allah is our highest hope."

This should be familiar as it is what Morsi said that night in Cairo during his speech at the university.

The Muslim Brotherhood seeks the resurrection of the wounded head. Nothing will satisfy but a caliphate that covers the entire globe; a revived Ottoman-style empire with the iron fisted rule of Shari'a.

And so, now, we cannot go back to sleep. It is time to be alert, awake and watching; ready to act to protect freedom for our children and grandchildren. Again, we have to *listen* to what they are saying. Across the globe they are saying "death to America!" They mean what they say. Believe it.

The Obama administration knows all of this. So why does it continuously try to convince the American people that many of the Islamist's are harmless? Instead, in September of 2012, our president proposed to eliminate a billion dollars of Egypt's $3 billion debt to the U.S. in order to help the new Muslim Brotherhood leadership of Egypt.[19]

Our leadership in Congress, by and large, and the administration are not taking the steps necessary to protect us from those who want an Islamic caliphate. There are only three possibilities for why this is: 1) They have their heads in the sand and don't want to face it; 2) They are naïve and don't understand the danger; 3) They know very well the plans and the danger and are allowing it to go forward anyway. It doesn't really matter which of the three applies to any particular elected official. If they aren't protecting our Constitution, our sovereignty, and our freedom, it's time to fire them.

In the next chapter, the implementation of the goals of the Muslim Brotherhood here in the U.S. will be discussed. You will see how these power hungry Islamic terrorists use what is called *Civilization Jihad* to achieve their ends.

2 - Civilization Jihad

"... we collectively believe that the state that was erected by the prophet in Medina was the ideal model for an Islamic state. The challenge today in the Islamic world is how do we accomplish this in our current era."
Imam, Feisal Abdul Rauf, aka, Imam of the Ground Zero Mosque[20]

The largest threat to the national security of the United States today is global Islamo-fascism. Islamic groups seeking to propagate Islam, as well as global Shari'a compliance, have the same end goal in mind; nothing but a global caliphate will do. The only thing that separates some of the various groups is the means they utilize to get there. Although this does not describe all Muslims, it does describe the violence and deception used over centuries to spread Islam.

Americans are very aware of what violent groups will do to see their goals met. We don't even have to go all the way back to 9/11 of 2001. We need only look to 9/11 in 2012 in Libya. Four Americans lost their lives at the hands of Islamist terrorists while the Obama administration removed their protection from Benghazi, did nothing to give aid during the attack and then claimed the attack was not a terrorist attack. Instead the attack was falsely attributed to have resulted from a "spontaneous" uprising caused by a very poorly produced video attacking the prophet Mohammad.

The Muslim Brotherhood

There are other groups who seek to restore the Caliphate by more stealthy methods. One of these groups is the Muslim Brotherhood.

Al-Qaeda Leader Ayman Al-Zawahiri said in September of 2012 in a video posted on Memri TV that Osama Bin Laden himself was a member of the Muslim Brotherhood on the Arabian Peninsula.[21] He left the organization over tactical differences. The Brotherhood has called its stealthy maneuvers to build a global caliphate, *Civilization Jihad*.

By now, many Americans are at least aware of the existence of the organization known as the Muslim Brotherhood. Despite claims from the Obama administration that the organization is largely secular and peaceful, the truth is quite to the contrary. The Muslim Brotherhood is a global organization of Islamists and Islamic organizations bent on establishing a global government with Islam and Shari'a Law at the core.

As noted in the previous chapter, the Muslim Brotherhood was founded by Hassan al-Banna, a 22 year old Egyptian school teacher. He asserted, "it is the nature of Islam to dominate, not to be dominated; to impose its laws on all nations and to extend its power to the entire planet."[22] That statement very clearly and simply sums up the philosophy and purpose behind the Muslim Brotherhood.

Al-Banna founded the organization in 1928 after the collapse of the Ottoman Empire and the eradication of the caliphate system that had prevailed in the Muslim world and which had united them for centuries. He believed Islam was not just a belief system but rather was meant to pervade every aspect of life from cradle to grave.

Since its founding, the Brotherhood has sought to propagate its brand of Islam worldwide, finding itself clashing even with other Muslims who do not hold to their "pure" faith. From the beginning, Al-Banna educated members, not only with a traditional Muslim education, but also in the way of Jihad. Remember what their creed is, "Allah is our objective. The prophet is our leader. The Qur'an is our law. Jihad is our way. Dying in the way of Allah is our highest hope."[23]

Hassan al-Banna knew that it would take a powerful global web of organizations all working together with total devotion of life and resources to see his goals come to fruition. To that end, he started organizations in a myriad of realms, including but not limited to:

economic, social, media, scouting, professional, governmental and military arenas.

The Muslim Brotherhood today has been very successful in establishing powerful organizations here in the U.S. They have also been very adept at getting their people into key positions within our government, educational institutions, our military, law enforcement, elected offices, to name a few. More in Chapter 4. The latter is actually a stated goal in a recently revealed secret Muslim Brotherhood document;

...the children of the American Ikhwani (Muslim Brotherhood) branch will have far-reaching impact and positions that make the ancestors proud.[24]

The Brotherhood knew, with the ever-increasing power of the United States of America there to stop them, they would never see the revival of the wounded head, the resurrection of the caliphate. The U.S. would have to be dealt with.

The Brotherhood Strategy

The document, *An Explanatory Memorandum On the General Strategic Goal for the Group In North America* was seized by the U.S. government in 2004 and used in the 2008 the Holy Land Foundation trial. Among other charges, the Foundation was on trial for providing material support to terrorists. The jury found against the Foundation on all 108 counts. The document is now readily available for anyone to read.[25]

The Memorandum clearly proves that the Muslim Brotherhood's goal and purpose in the United States is to "settle" *our* country for Islam and impose Shari'a Law.

For Al-Banna, the first phase of infiltration was to saturate the country they were settling with as many mosques and Islamic centers as possible. For Muslims, symbolism is extremely important. During the years of the caliphates they would build a mosque in a show of strength and domination over the defeated people after they conquered a nation or territory. One such time that this took place was with the conquering of most of Spain and the establishment of the Caliphate of

Córdoba. Big on symbolism, the Mosque at Ground zero was to be called the Cordoba Center.

Critics can say all they want that the cleric who wants to build this Mosque is innocent and harmless. The facts don't back that up. Just like in Spain; they came, they conquered, they built a mosque as a symbol of their victory. The community center part of the effort was renamed Park51 to hide the Cordoba link to Spain, but the interfaith portion is still called Cordoba even though the name is not used publicly. Although about 4,000 square feet has been renovated, because of lawsuits and other roadblocks, the planned center has never been built.

The Brotherhood's *Memorandum* clearly states;

* Settlement: "That Islam and its Movement become a part of the homeland it lives in".
* Establishment: "That Islam turns into firmly-rooted organizations on whose bases civilization, structure and testimony are built".
* Stability: "That Islam is stable in the land on which its people move".
* Enablement: "That Islam is enabled within the souls, minds and the lives of the people of the country in which it moves".
* Rooting: "That Islam is resident and not a passing thing, or rooted "entrenched" in the soil of the spot where it moves and not a strange plant to it."[26]

In spite of this, Secretary of State Hillary Clinton called the Muslim Brotherhood "peaceful" and "nonviolent."[27] Even more shocking from their *Memorandum*:

Understanding the role of the Muslim Brother in North America. The process of settlement is a "Civilization-Jihadist Process" with all the word means. The Ikhwan must understand that their work in America is a kind of grand Jihad in eliminating and destroying the Western civilization from within and "sabotaging" it's miserable house by their hands and the hands of the believers so that it is eliminated and God's religion is made victorious over all other religions. Without this level of understanding, we are not up to this challenge and have not prepared ourselves for Jihad yet. It is a Muslim's destiny to perform Jihad and work wherever he is and wherever he lands until the final hour comes, and there is no escape from that destiny except for those who chose to slack. But, would the slackers and the Mujahedeen be equal?[28]

A fatwa issued in 2003 by key spiritual advisor to the Brotherhood, Sheik Yusuf al-Qaradawi, described how Islam would defeat Europe by exploiting western liberalism and democracy, "...it is eminently clear that the future belongs to Islam, and that the religion of Allah will be victorious and will, by the grace of Allah, conquer all other religions."[29] Qaradawi said that it would be made possible by spreading Islam until it was strong enough to take over the entire continent. The Brotherhood is implementing the same strategy here in the U.S.

The Brotherhood is shockingly far along in their schemes.

Phases of the World Underground Movement Plan

Another Brotherhood document lays out the plan for their *Civilization Jihad* in the United States. Called *Phases of the World Underground Movement Plan*, it was taken from the home of Ismael Elbarasse by the FBI in Virginia in 2004, along with a multitude of other documents. The phases are outlined as:

Phase One: Discreet and secret establishment of leadership.

Phase Two: Phase of gradual appearance on the public scene and exercising and utilizing various public activities. It [the MB] greatly succeeded in implementing this stage. It also succeeded in achieving a great deal of its important goals, such as infiltrating various sectors of the government.

Phase Three: Escalation phase, prior to conflict and confrontation with the rulers, through utilizing mass media. Currently in progress. In just one instance, the Islamic Circle of North America is currently in the midst of a $3 million campaign to promote Shari'a.

Phase Four: Open public confrontation with the Government through exercising the political pressure approach. The Muslim Brotherhood is aggressively implementing the above-mentioned approach. One effort is to train members on the use of weapons domestically and overseas in anticipation of zero-hour. It has noticeable activities in this regard.

Phase Five: Seizing power to establish their Islamic Nation under which all parties and Islamic groups are united.[30]

In 2010, Al Qaeda published an open letter in their *Inspire* magazine issuing a challenge to the Muslim Brotherhood. Al Qaeda was in a full court press demanding that it was time to move past stealth in Islamic countries that weren't Shari'a compliant and were consorting with "infidel" nations.

Key to note in this revelation is that stealthy, non-violent *Civilization Jihad* only remains so until the Islamists deem violence necessary. Remember, these are not fringe elements. These people are movers and shakers wielding real power both here and internationally. We ignore them at our peril.

Ongoing Efforts

Frank Gaffney, Assistant Secretary of Defense under President Reagan has outlined the stealth phases of *Civilization Jihad* in greater detail at his site, muslimbrotherhoodinamerica.com:

1. Keep the infidels ignorant of the true nature and progress of Shari'a. This requires Information Dominance. After the 9/11 Commission Report was published in 2004, Islamic organizations demanded the words that offend them be removed from public documents. The government complied across the board. Nine hundred pages were stripped from the FBI training manual and these terms can no longer be used: Islam, Muslim, Jihad, enemy, Muslim Brotherhood, Hamas, Hezbollah, al Qaeda, caliphate, Shari'a law.
2. Prohibit, or at least discourage blasphemy and slander against Islam, Allah, Mohammed, and their followers.

The OIC (Organization of the Islamic Conference) is enforcing Information Dominance. The **Cairo Declaration on Human Rights in Islam (CDHRI)** is a declaration of the member states of the Organization of the Islamic Conference adopted in Cairo in 1990. It gives an overview on the Islamic perspective on human rights, and affirms Islamic Shari'a as its sole source.

On March 25, 2010, the Defamation of Religion resolution passed the UN's human rights council, resolution #A/HRC/13/L.1.[31] A similar resolution passed in 2011 with language like "defamation" removed making it less offensive to proponents of freedom as resolution 16/18.[32]

Although it was temporarily shelved at the UN general assembly in September, 2012, the OIC will not be giving up any time soon. They do not see this newest resolution as having replaced that which they have been pursuing fervently for so many years. On the contrary, they affirm their dedication to see their original goals through to fruition. In a document produced by the OIC, they have clearly stated what they want:

The OIC:
Affirms categorically the firm determination of Member States to continue their effective cooperation and close consultations to combat Islamophobia, defamation of all divine religions, and incitement to hatred, hostility and discrimination against Muslims;

Furthermore, the OIC:

Calls upon all States to prevent any advocacy of religious discrimination, hostility or violence and defamation of Islam by incorporating legal and administrative measures which render defamation illegal and punishable by law, and also urges all Member States to adopt specific and relevant educational measures at all levels.

The OIC has pushed this strategy relentlessly at the **international level for more than a decade. The OIC, the largest international**

organization next to the UN, is Saudi based and is basically a religious arm whose major practical purpose for the past decade has been to combat defamation of Islam. Twenty percent of Saudi Arabia's national budget goes toward the expansion of Islam. Saudi Arabia is a religiously restricted nation where a Muslim can face death for leaving Islam.

This is serious. The U.S. Commission on International Religious Freedom has stated:

> In recent years, USCIRF has been seriously concerned about initiatives by some UN member states to create an international legal norm, or redefine existing norms, to protect religions, rather than individuals, from alleged "defamation." Instead of helping to address religious persecution and discrimination, as its proponents allege, a global ban on the so-called "defamation of religions" would exacerbate these problems and undermine fundamental individual rights, including religious freedom and free expression. Essentially, it would be an international blasphemy law.[33]

Gaffney provides further examples of how the U.S. has fallen victim to this Islamic agenda:

3. Demand Concession
   - 2006: Metropolitan Airport Authority, Minneapolis-St. Paul: a cab driver can refuse to service the blind because of their dogs which are seen by many Muslims as unclean.
   - Foot baths and prayer rooms in public places at taxpayer expense.
   - Triumphalist Mosques and Islamic Centers

4. Utilize Educational Vehicles
   - Penetrate and subvert school systems
   - Establishing Islamic Charter Schools
   - Skewing Textbooks
   - Using Curricula to proselytize
   - Enforcing with testing, favoritism toward Islam

- Insinuating Islamic Speakers
- Money to Universities to set up Middle East Studies Departments
    - Appointing anti-American professors
    - Giving scholarships to students

5. Subvert institutions through one-sided interfaith dialogue (They do not intend to build bridges. Their faith requires them to bring all to Islam. It is a ONE-WAY bridge!)
    - Interfaith Seminars, panels, services
    - Borrowing Christian churches and synagogues for Muslim worship
    - Condemnation of Islamophobia
    - Prohibiting defamation of religion
    - Enlisting support for mosque building
    - Touting shared faith traditions, practices
    - Interfaith excursions

A group of Muslim leaders sent an open letter to the leaders of the Christian churches in America. This was the collective response of the recipients. *Loving God and Neighbor Together; A Christian response to 'A Common Word Between Us and You.'* The problem with this document is that it claims we all, Muslims and Christians alike serve the same "one God," and that we must engage in "interfaith dialogue between us, for our common ground is that on which hangs all the Law and the Prophets (Matthew 22:40)."[34] This "interfaith dialogue" is for "those who seek each other's good, for the one God unceasingly seeks our good."[35]

The 'Common Word' document was signed by over 300 church leaders including Rick Warren and Bill Hybels. While it is important for Christians to reach out in love to all Muslims, they must be aware of the goals of groups like the Muslim Brotherhood which try to force us, our children and our grandchildren into the iron grip of Shari'a.

The god of Islam and the God of Christianity are not the same entity. The inscription on the ceiling inside the Dome of the Rock, a prime Muslim monument which stands in Jerusalem clearly states:

O People of the Book! Do not exaggerate in your religion nor utter aught concerning God save the truth. The Messiah, Jesus son of Mary, was only a Messenger of God, and His Word which He conveyed unto Mary, and a spirit from Him. So believe in God and His messengers, and say not 'Three' - Cease! (it is) better for you! - God is only One God. Far be it removed from His transcendent majesty that He should have a son. ... Whoso disbelieveth the revelations of God (will find that) lo! God is swift at reckoning![36]

Gaffney's exposé continues:

6. Shari'a Compliant Finance; already, financial institutions in the U.S. must hire Shari'a authorities to determine whether a transaction is Shari'a compliant or not. (Note: A name you will recognize by now, Sheik Yusuf al-Qaradawi, is one of the most preeminent Shari'a compliant finance industry's advisors. He is paid handsomely to advise. Under Shari'a, at least 1/8 of zakat (one of the 5 pillars of Islam which concerns financial giving) must go to support Jihad. Qaradawi surely adheres to zakat. For the institutions who utilize his advisory services, this constitutes material support for terrorism.

The world's largest purveyor of Shari'a-compliant insurance products was purchased in 2008 by the federal government with tax money; AIG. Over $1 billion went directly into the company's Shari'a compliant division.)

7. Place Muslim Brothers into positions from which they can exercise influence. (This will be discussed at length in Chapter 4.)

Each of these stealth stages are running concurrently – very successfully. These plans have been known by our government for several years now. The question remains, why does our leadership pave the way for the Islamists? It has been reported that Obama has enlisted Qaradawi in secret talks between the U.S. and the Taliban.[37]

Rashad Hussain, President Obama's Special Envoy to The Organization of Islamic Cooperation, met with Qaradawi envoy Abdallah bin Bayyah, and well known Muslim Brotherhood leader in his own right. The meeting was supposedly to discuss the rights of religious minorities.[38] That cannot possibly be taken seriously when the Muslim Brotherhood seeks to eradicate the entire planet of all other religions but their version of Islam.

Obama Supporting Islamist Activity

Our President devoted half his speech at the UN in the fall of 2012 to the grievances of the Muslim world, saying among other statements, "The future must not belong to those who slander the prophet of Islam."[39] At best, this is hypocritical. Obama's view of Christianity has turned the Biblical definition upside down. The Democratic Party even rejected putting God into its platform three times at the 2012 Democrat Convention!

In 2010, Charles Boden, NASA administrator told Al Jazeera that when he accepted his position, Obama charged him with 3 tasks:

> One, he wanted me to help re-inspire children to want to get into science and math; [second], he wanted me to expand our international relationships; and third, and perhaps foremost, he wanted me to find a way to reach out to the Muslim world and engage much more with dominantly Muslim nations to help them feel good about their historic contribution to science and engineering — science, math and engineering. [40]

President Obama is turning NASA into a vehicle for Muslim outreach... why?

Currently the scandal in Libya proves further that the administration will do anything NOT to confront Islamic terrorism. Obama, Hillary Clinton and even the head of the CIA, had initially all publicly blamed the badly produced short film, *The Innocence of Muslims* for the outbreak of violence that caused the death of four Americans in Libya, including Ambassador Chris Stevens.

The Benghazi attacks were carried out by Islamic militants. The truth surrounding all of the things that were taking place in Libya is slowly but surely coming out. What we are left with is another attack on Americans by Jihadists and an administration that was caught red-handed removing security in Libya, not providing aid once the attack was underway, and then lying about what motivated the attack. The unclassified report from an independent review panel was damning and laid the blame squarely on "systematic failures and leadership... deficiencies" that left the security at the Benghazi Special Mission "grossly inadequate."[41]

Less than 10 days following the deaths of the four Americans, including the Ambassador to Libya, Chris Stevens, Sheikh Abu Mundhir Al-Shinqiti issued a fatwa approving the killing of the U.S. ambassador and the others and called for the deaths of more American ambassadors.[42] This is the kind of Jihad we are facing, from the top down within the Muslim hierarchy. We are past the point where the argument can realistically be made that the leadership of our nation does not know the nature and scope of this Jihad against us.

The question then becomes, "Why is the Obama administration doing all they can to allow Islamists into American politics and culture?" It can be only one of three reasons; 1) Obama is a Muslim (or possibly an Islamist/activist) himself as has been suggested by many researchers (more on this later), 2) He is a progressive liberal whose ideology has been shown for over a hundred years to blind adherents to reality, or 3) He is a progressive ideologue who wants to destroy America, and is using radical Islam as one tool to do it. There really isn't any other possibility. No rational American would ever knowingly invite radical Islam into America knowing their plan is to destroy America as we have known it.

In the next chapter, the infiltration in key areas of the Obama Administration by Saudi Wahhabi Islam will be discussed and its role in the spread of radical Islam and financing of Islamic terrorism.

3 - Wahhabi Islam: The Royal Puppet Masters

Saudi activities include the building and the support of mosques, religious schools and Islamic centers that propagate the very extreme Wahhabist Islam coming out of Saudi Arabia.
United States Commission on International Religious Freedom

Many in the West, and especially in America, are still holding to the claim that the Muslim Brotherhood is a moderate, largely secular, and peace-loving organization. The leaders in the U.S. who are chanting this mantra are either incredibly naïve and uninformed, simply not understanding the Islamic Eastern mind; or, more likely, they are outright liars. The long hidden goals of the Brotherhood have been revealed and should move every freedom lover to action.

What we are experiencing since 9/11 with al Qaeda and other terrorist groups is partly because of "blowback," the natural consequence, of the U.S.' practice of working with radicals. Our government allied itself with the most radical, militant Afghan mujahedeen, training and arming them, in the fight against the Soviets. And more recently, it is being revealed that the U.S. worked in much the same way as in Afghanistan in the 1980's with members of the Libyan Muslim Brotherhood in order to oust Qaddafi.[43]

The primary goal of the Brotherhood in the West is to establish an Islamic Shari'a-based infrastructure that they can put into place to rule when the time is right. This is not a secret. Anyone with a computer and an internet connection can easily discover these facts. So why is it that our government continues to not only dialogue with members of the Muslim Brotherhood, but to give them key positions of influence?

Saudi Arabia—Birthplace of Wahhabism

One nation stands out as home base for the global Islamic mischief; that is Saudi Arabia. Hillary Clinton has stated that Saudis are the largest financiers of terrorism. A December 2009 classified memo from Secretary of State Hillary Clinton indicated donors in Saudi Arabia were "the most significant source" of funding to Wahhabist terrorist groups, including al-Qaeda.[44]

The Wahhabist form of Islam is considered by its adherents to be the purest form. Founded by Muhammad bin Abd al-Wahhab, a Salafi Islamist[a] Theologian in the 1700's, it is a very radical form of Islam which considers all who don't follow it, including Muslims who follow other branches of Islam, to be heathens and enemies.

Osama bin Laden and the Muslim Brotherhood both have their roots in Wahhabist Saudi Arabia. Furthermore, recall that fifteen of the nineteen 9/11 terrorists were from Saudi Arabia. This brand of Islam seeks to conquer all other religions through whatever means necessary—including all other sects of Islam.

The United States Commission on International Religious Freedom (USCirf) once again recommends Saudi Arabia be designated by the State Department as a *Country of Particular Concern* (CPC). The following is from that 337 page report issued in March of 2012:

> More than 10 years since the September 11, 2001 attacks on the United States, the Saudi government has failed to implement a number of promised reforms related to promoting freedom of thought, conscience, and religion or belief. The Saudi government persists in banning all forms of public religious expression other than that of the government's own interpretation of one school of [Wahhabi] Islam; prohibits churches, synagogues, temples, and other non-Muslim places of worship; uses in its schools and posts online state textbooks that continue to espouse intolerance and incite violence; and periodically interferes with private religious practice.[45]

---

[a] The Salaf, are the earliest predecessors of what these Wahhabi Islamists, salafist theologians, pass on what they consider to be the only truly pure form of Islam.

The report further states that the Saudis continue to practice and promote activities globally which serve to exacerbate extremist action and ideology. These activities include the building and the support of mosques, religious schools and Islamic centers that propagate the very extreme Wahhabist Islam coming out of Saudi Arabia.[46]

The USCirf report also expresses concern for the vast numbers of Muslim clerics who are coming out of schools in Pakistan and Saudi Arabia which teach this politico-religious ideology which seeks global domination and promotes hatred for, and violence against, non-Muslims.[47]

Others such as Shia, Ahmadi, and Ismaili Muslims are often violently persecuted, many having been detained, beaten and even be-headed while visiting Saudi Arabia performing Hajj, or pilgrimage. The Saudi government uses their rigid apostasy and blasphemy laws to persecute anyone they choose.[48]

The 1998 International Religious Freedom Act (IRFA) mandated the promotion of religious liberty around the world as a central element of American foreign policy. The IRFA provides the standard for a CPC (Country of Particular Concern) designation. It requires for such designation that the particular government has "engaged in or tolerated particularly severe violations of religious freedom," which are defined as "systematic, ongoing, egregious violations of religious freedom."[49]

The U.S. can exercise influence on CPC's to bring about compliance with USCirf standards such as employing economic sanctions. In spite of blatant human rights violations, Saudi Arabia continues to get waivers on any kind of action that might bring about real change ever since 2006, two years after it was first designated a Country of Particular Concern.

Ali al Ahmed, a Shia Muslim living in Saudi Arabia, in an interview with PBS' *Frontline* described what it is like for a non- Wahhabist in that country;

> [Regarding the Saudi government:] It's intolerant toward other Muslims who are not Salafis. (Wahhabist) You can see a book that is printed [by] a branch of Imam, Imam Muhammad

Ibn Saud University in Washington area, and they printed this book where they say that 95 percent of Muslims are [merely] claimant to Islam [They are not considered real Muslims]. If you don't believe in Salafi, you are not a human being. You are something of a lower grade, that you can be persecuted or hurt, and it is OK, accepted, in that ideology. It's accepted to be killed, or maimed... The religious authority in Saudi Arabia controls the justice system. This is very important. ... All the judges in Saudi Arabia are Salafi.

They control all education. Saudi Arabia private and public schools, their curriculum is prescribed by the government. The religious curriculums are written and monitored and taught by Salafi Saudis only. Well, here, this is a book, Hadeeth, for ninth grade. Hadeeth is a statement of Prophet Mohammed. "The day of judgment will not arrive until Muslims fight Jews, and Muslim will kill Jews until the Jew hides behind a tree or a stone. Then the tree and the stone will say, 'Oh Muslim, oh, servant of God, this is a Jew behind me. Come and kill him'." This is taught for 14-year-old boys in Saudi Arabia. This is a book printed by Saudi government Ministry of Education.[50]

Ali al Ahmed went on to make this blunt and shocking statement:

Because the hijackers, 15 hijackers who are Saudis, they studied this thinking–destructive thinking–in Saudi Arabia. They spent a few months in Afghanistan. But they lived their life, they studied this in government mosques. They studied this kind of curriculum that I talked to you about. ... Government curriculum inspired what happened in New York. ...there is an (sic) another fatwa by a government official, who is still working for the government, who said the same thing: that Jihad should be waged against Shi'a. So the hate message ... that some Salafi carries, started against it locally ... until it reached New York.[51]

We cannot afford to forget that the only difference between the seemingly peaceful members of the Muslim Brotherhood and the 9/11 murderers is tactics. They have the same endgame in mind.

9/11 Inconsistencies

President George W. Bush frequently promised to use the power of the U.S. to stop the flow of money to militant Islamists, all the while pledging to hold financers of terrorism just as responsible as those who pulled the triggers. In fact, the access of members of the Muslim Brotherhood to positions of power actually *increased*, both in number and scope of influence, under Bush's leadership.

President Bush went out guns blazing to get the ones who attacked us. At least that is what we were supposed to believe. In reality, the Bush administration failed to target many of the backers of the terrorists, especially those with Saudi connections.

The Rabita Trust is one organization which happened to be targeted. Designated a "Global Terrorist Entity" its assets were frozen one month after the 9/11 attacks. However, its founder, Saudi born, Abdullah Omar Naseef has escaped accountability. Organizations are made up of individuals. *Individuals* like Naseef were never held accountable.

Naseef, has powerful friends in high places. One of his well-placed associates is Huma Abedin, a deputy chief of staff and aide to Hillary Clinton. She was once part of Naseef's organization, the Institute of Muslim Minority Affairs (IMMA). (There will be more on Huma in the next chapter.)

In the days following the 9/11 attacks, air travel was severely restricted because of national security. Craig Unger reported in the *New York Times* that 300 Saudis left the U.S. with the apparent clearance of the Bush White House. Two dozen of those leaving our country were members of Osama bin Laden's family.[52]

One of those permitted to leave was Prince Turki bin Faisal, the widely feared head of the Saudi Intelligence Agency, until he was abruptly fired in August of 2001, just days before the 9/11 attacks. His replacement was officially announced on August 31. This begs the question asked so pointedly by Walid Shoebat[53] in his investigative report on these events, "What, exactly, was the longtime head of Saudi Arabia's secret police doing in the United States, while 15 young Saudis were carrying out their attacks?"[54]

Walid Shoebat is a former radicalized PLO terrorist. He is one of the founders of the Forum for Middle East Understanding, and is a well-connected expert on the Middle East. As a Palestinian/ American growing up mostly in the Middle East, and as former Muslim terrorist himself, he understands the Islamist mind.[55] He was transformed into a Christian after reading the Bible and now works to expose the evil underpinnings of Islam.

The 9/11 hijackers made at least six trips to Las Vegas. Prince Turki flew with more than 30 others out of Vegas just a few days after the attacks. This Saudi prince had documented connections to Osama bin Laden and Pakistan's Inter Service Intelligence, which propped up the Taliban, yet the Bush Administration allowed them to leave from Las Vegas. None of them were interviewed.[56] Inexplicably, Turki later became the Saudi Ambassador to the U.S.

So many questions remain since 9/11. It has been reported that names of key Saudis were scrubbed from the 9/11 Commission's report. The captured number three man in al Qaeda, Abu Zubaydah, named three Saudi Princes as intermediaries when he was interrogated by the U.S.; Prince Ahmed bin Salman bin Abdulaziz, Prince Sultan bin Faisal bin Turki bin Abdullah, and Prince Ahmed bin Salman bin Abdul Aziz. Zubaydah was a leading member of Osama bin Laden's organization involved with the operational control of al-Qaeda's millennium bomb plots, as well as the attack on the USS Cole.[57]

Johanna McGeary wrote in *Time Magazine* that after Zubaydah was captured in Pakistan, he was transferred to Afghanistan where he was sedated with sodium pentothal. Intending to intimidate the prisoner, what they found in Zubaydah's reaction "was not fear, but utter relief."[58]

During the interrogation, Zubaydah was falsely told he was being held in Saudi Arabia and that his interrogators, two Arab Americans, were actually Saudis. McGeary reports that he was happy to see 'Saudi agents.' Seeming relieved, he rattled off phone numbers of the three princes named above. He said these princes were senior members of the Saudi royal family and would "tell you what to do."[59]

All three of the princes named by Zubaydah met untimely ends under suspicious circumstances a few months after Zubaydah's capture and within a week of each other. The Bush administration had warned the Saudis that they would take matters into their own hands. One administration official was quoted as saying, "We don't care how you deal with the problem; just do it or we will."[60]

A detailed report of the Saudi Princes' deaths was written by Walid Shoebat and Ben Barrack. The first prince, young and healthy, died of an alleged heart attack during routine surgery. The second died in a reported car accident on his way to the first prince's funeral.[61] The third died of thirst in the desert, or so they say. With great discernment, Barrack and Shoebat call into question the reported events:

- Three princes named by Abu Zubaydah as having helped plan 9/11 all die mysteriously within four months of Zubaydah's capture and within one week of each other.
- The stories of these three princes are not included in the 9/11 Commission Report nor are they available in the original Arabic media sources.
- There are no photos or verifiable names of individuals present during these deaths.
- The third prince dies after leaving behind a functioning mobile phone and walking through the desert without water, before dying next to the car he left to find help.[62]

The details of the deaths of these three men do not add up. A reading of the complete Shoebat article is very enlightening.

While this evidence is of concern, it pales in significance to the complex network of Islamist organizations and individuals that have been deliberately allowed into the most sensitive positions within the Obama administration.

4 – Islamic Networking to Penetrate and Influence

" The Muslim call to prayer
is one of the purest sounds on earth at sunset."
Barack Hussein Obama, March 6, 2007[63]

The Obama administration has put out a virtual red carpet for terrorists according to The Investigative Project On Terrorism. This organization sifted through reams of White House visitor logs to document hundreds of visits by Islamic radicals to the White House.[64] The following are just a few of the Islamists welcomed into the Obama White House:

- Hussam Ayloush – executive director of CAIR's Los Angeles office. CAIR is listed an unindicted co-conspirator[65] in the Holy Land Foundation Trial.[b] This designation was easily upheld by U.S. District Court Judge Jorge Solis who later ruled that ample evidence had been produced that linked CAIR to Hamas. Ayloush attended at least two White House meetings.[66]

---

[b] Calling itself America's largest Islamic charity, Holy Land Foundation (HLF) purported to be a source of help for needy Palestinian Muslims in Israel, Jordan, Lebanon, and the Palestinian Authority (PA). In reality, however, the Foundation was a major financier of the terrorist organization Hamas. HLF's precursor, the Occupied Land Fund, was named in a May 1991 Muslim Brotherhood document – titled "An Explanatory Memorandum on the General Strategic Goal for the Group in North America" – as one of the Brotherhood's 29 likeminded "organizations of our friends" that shared the common goal of destroying America and turning it into a Muslim nation. Seven defendants (plus numerous individuals that should have been indicted but weren't), were tried but the trial ended in a mistrial on Oct. 22, 2007. After a retrial, the jury convicted five former HLF officials.
(See http://www.discoverthenetworks.org/printgroupProfile.asp?grpid=6181)

- Louay Safi – formerly executive director of the Islamic Society of North America, ISNA, visited the White House twice. ISNA is another unindicted co-conspirator in the Holy Land Foundation Trial and is a front organization for the Muslim Brotherhood.[67]
- Esam Omeish – former head of the Muslim American Society, created by the Muslim Brotherhood, visited the White House three times.[68]
- Muzammil Siddiqi – former president of ISNA, visited the White House at least once in 2010. Siddiqi supports laws in nations where homosexuality is punishable by death while at the same time claiming to oppose violence.[69]
- Rashad Hussain – is the American ambassador to the 52 nation Organization of the Islamic Conference and is closely aligned with the Muslim Brotherhood. Prior to joining the White House as a lawyer, he defended Brotherhood leaders like Sami al-Arain. He is an avid proponent of Islam and even claims that "Islam rejects violent extremism."[70]

Many more Islamists, albeit with lower profiles were afforded access as well during Obama's first term;

- Farhana Khera – executive director of Muslim Advocates and the National Association of Muslim Lawyers (NAML)[71]
- Hisham al-Talib – A founder and current VP of Finance for the International Institute of Islamic Thought (IIIT)[72]
- Imam Talib El-Hajj Abdur Rashid – religious and spiritual leader of Harlem's Mosque of the Islamic Brotherhood, he has defended Mahmoud Ahmadinejad and is also an activist seeking the release of Imam Jamil Abdullah al-Amin who was convicted of killing a Georgia police officer in 2002.[73]
- Hatem Abudayyeh – executive director of the Chicago-based Arab American Action Network, said in a 2006 interview "The U.S. and Israel will continue to describe Hamas, Hezbollah and the other Palestinian and Lebanese resistance organizations as "terrorists," but the real terrorists are the governments and military forces of the U.S. and Israel."[74] Yet he was still welcomed into the Obama White House.[75]

Islamists in Key Positions of Power

Islamist activity within the Obama Administration goes much deeper than whatever went on in these various meetings. Individuals with close ties to the Muslim Brotherhood have achieved positions throughout all levels even to the highest level within our government. This was well underway during the Bush Administration, but has exploded exponentially during Obama's reign. In reading this, remember the writings of Islamic scholars it is forbidden to give oath and allegiance to more than one leader. They obey one master – Allah.

In previous chapters, the case was carefully and effectively made that the Muslim Brotherhood seeks nothing less than world domination. First, they want to rid the Middle East of Western influence. Second, they want to rid the West of Western influence. Don't forget what has been uncovered in their own documents:

"The Iquan (Muslim Brotherhood) must understand their work in America is a kind of grand Jihad, in eliminating and destroying the Western Civilization from within and sabotaging its *miserable house by their hands and the hands of the believers so* that it is eliminated and god's religion is made victorious."[76]

The abbreviated list of individuals discussed in this section have secured their role in advancing the Muslim Brotherhood's *Civilization Jihad* and are having a major effect on policy.

Huma and Saleha Abedin

Huma Mahmood Abedin (born 1976) was an American deputy chief of staff and aide to former U.S. Secretary of State Hillary Rodham Clinton. She was chief of staff for Clinton during her bid for the presidency. How Huma was ever vetted and permitted anywhere near a former first lady is a mystery. According to an impressively documented special report by Walid Shoebat:[77]

Hassan Abedin, Huma's brother, held a fellowship for several years under the supervision of Sheikh Yusuf al-Qaradawi, along with Abdullah Omar Naseef, the founder of "Rabita Trust", a Specially Designated Global Terrorist Entity by the U.S. Naseef has been the Chairman of the Board and Qaradawi a Board member. Hassan's Brotherhood ties are undeniable. For more than two years prior to Huma serving on Naseef's board, Naseef was formally connected to Al-Qaeda by the U.S. Government.

Huma's mother, Saleha Abedin, is a member of the Muslim Sisterhood. Among other roles she is a professor of sociology at King Abdulaziz University Women's College, Jeddah, Saudi Arabia. She also founded Dar Al-Hekma College in Jeddah, along with Yaseen Abdullah Kadi who has been designated a terrorist by the United States. Huma arranged for Hillary Clinton to speak at Dar Al-Hekma in 2010. We have already established in Chapter 3 that Wahhabi Islam reigns supreme in Saudi Arabia, especially in educational institutions.

Saleha has also been chairwoman with the International Islamic Committee for Woman and Child (IICWC). They deleted evidence of this when Huma faced scrutiny as her Muslim Brotherhood connections were called into question, but Walid's organization captured the pages before they were pulled down from the internet. The IICWC operates under the Muslim World League, therefore its policies and practices would be set by Muslim Brotherhood leaders. The draft of the IICWC charter states: (translated from Arabic; the English versions are sanitized)

"That is the message of this Charter, which the International Islamic Committee for Woman and Child of the World Islamic Call and Relief, completed its draft of which participated in the preparation over the three years the eminent scientists: a. Dr. Ahmed El-Assal, Dr. Ahmed Mahdi Abdul Halim, Dr. Jamal Eddine Attia, Dr. Salah Abdel-Mut'al, Dr. Abdul Rahman Al-Naqib, Dr. Abdul Latif Amer, Dr. Ali Gomaa, Dr. Fathi Lashin, Dr. Mohamed Emara, Dr. Imam Mohammed Kamal al-Din, Dr. Makarem al-Dairi, Dr. Yusuf al-Qaradawi."[78]

Many of these individuals are key leaders in the Brotherhood.

An Egyptian newspaper, Masr, had this to say about the IICWC (Shoebat provides a translation):

"The Islamic Committee for Woman and Child condemns passing any law that imprisons a husband under the pretext of raping his wife or to have sex with her without her consent as prescribed under 'marital rape'. The Committee, at the end of the workshop, which was held in Cairo regarding the Charter of the Family in Islam, rejected any law that gives women the freedom to control her body, or the recognition of illegitimate children. The committee is steadfast in stressing male superiority over women including the necessity of a woman to obey her husband. It refuses to grant gays any rights or abolish differences between men and women."[79] (Feb 22, 2009)

Another group to which the organization which Saleha Abedin chairs belongs is the IICDR (International Islamic Council for Daw'a and Relief). It is likely she belongs to it personally. There is a Dr. S. Abdien listed, and Anglicized versions of non-English words and names often have multiple possible spellings.[c] Regardless, Saleha is chairwoman of one of the organizations tied to the IICDR.

The IICDR coordinates more than one hundred Islamic NGO's and GO's all over the world from its headquarters in Cairo - Egypt. Presidency Staff Council consists of H.E Sheikh AL Azhar - President, H.E. Marshal Abdel Rahman Sowar AL Dahap - Vice President, H.E.AL Sheikh Yousf AL Hegy - Vice President, H.E. Dr. Abdulah Salih AL Obeid, Vice President, H.E. Prof. Kamel AL Sharif, Secretary General, and Excellencies Presidents of Specialized Committee in the council among them Dr. Abdullah Nasif (IICI) Mr. Abdulmalik AL Hamar, (IICHR) Dr. S. Abdien (IICW&CH) Hamid A. AL-Rifaie, President of (IIFD).

Another connection held by both Huma's mother and her late father Sayed Abedin is in their administration of The Institute of Muslim

---

[c] The reader will note that in print for example, the new President of Egypt is listed as Mursi, and Morsi almost equally. The name Mohammed also has many different English versions.

Minority Affairs. The details of the founding of this organization differ depending on whether the source is in English, or Arabic. Arabic sources say that Naseef founded the IMMA in Great Britain and Saudi Arabia and entrusted Huma's parents with leading it with Mr. Abedin being the chief editor. The man charged with managing the IMMA was Ahmed Ba-Hafth-Allah, who was the General Trustee for the World Assembly of Muslim Youth (WAMY). This is what Walid has to say about WAMY:

> The connections between Ba-Hifth-Allah and WAMY are quite extensive as well. This places Naseef at the center of both the IMMA and WAMY, another group with multiple connections to Muslim Brotherhood entities. According to Discover the Networks, Osama bin Laden's nephew—Abdullah bin Laden—incorporated WAMY three blocks away from where four of the 9/11 hijackers lived prior to the attacks. The more notorious bin Laden was allegedly funding militants in the Philippines through WAMY. In a Romanian newspaper report, WAMY was identified as a group that heavily funded a Muslim Brotherhood organization that operated under alternate names. WAMY has also welcomed speakers such as Tariq Ramadan, Rashid Gannouchi, and Hamas leader Khaled Mash'al. WAMY's funds have reportedly wound up in the hands of Hamas on several occasions. In an article published in the Washington Post, a Senior Customs Special Agent signed an affidavit that claims a WAMY publication said the following: "The Jews are humanity's enemies: they foment immorality in this world."[80]

Huma herself was connected to Naseef when she served with his organization, the IMMA, as an Assistant Editor from at least December 2, 2002 to September 24, 2008. She left to accept her position with Hillary Clinton.

In 1978, the Abedins frequently communicated with Maulana Muhammad Yousuf a member of the Tabligh, which is the equivalent of the Muslim Brotherhood in the region of India with the same ideology, and extensive ties to al-Qaeda and other terrorist groups. He was also a member of Jamaat-e-Islami, an Islamist political party.

More recently, the Jamaat has expressed support for violent Jihad against American forces and supports the Jihad of groups like Hamas and Hezbollah.

Huma Abedin is indeed very closely connected to those deeply rooted in Salafist organizations; as close as her sibling and both parents, just as Congresswoman Michelle Bachman expressed with justifiable concern. Bachmann was viciously attacked by various Islamists and the Obama administration for her efforts at exposing the truth. More on that later.

Dr. Abdullah Nasif

Notice one of the members of the IICDR is one Dr. Abdullah Nasif (Also spelled Naseef). As documented previously, his organization funded the Rabita Trust which was the financial arm in the U.S. of the Muslim World League. Recall that the Rabita Trust, was designated by the U.S. government as a "Global Terrorist Entity" and had its assets frozen one month after 9/11. Naseef has escaped accountability yet most American people don't even know who he is. Naseef was also involved in the SAAR/SAFA charity group which will be discussed later. The Rabita Trust still exists, reorganized and renamed, Rabita al-Alam al-Islami, and Saleha Abedin is a member of this organization. This is just scratching the surface of Saleha Abedin's close Muslim Brotherhood connections.[81]

We have barely touched on the connections Walid Shoebat has exposed. A thorough reading of his expose is highly recommended.[82]

Mohamed Elibiary

Next we will look at Mohamed Elibiary who founded the Freedom and Justice Foundation in Dallas. In 2010, he was appointed to the Homeland Security Advisory Council in October 2010. He spoke at a December 2004 seminar in honor of Iran's Ayatollah Ruhollah Khomeini, titled *A Tribute to the Great Islamic Visionary*. When he came under public scrutiny for his attendance at that event, he insisted that he didn't know the purpose of the meeting and was unaware of the Ayatollah's views. He would have had to been trapped in a cave for decades to be unaware of Khomeini's views. Yet, his excuse was not challenged.

Elibiary argued in an op-ed against the assassination of terrorist Anwar al-Awlaki, denying his role in inspiring Jihad, even though it is documented that al-Awlaki was a mentor to many Jihadists and a leader of al-Qaeda where he died in Yemen. While the authors agree that there was no question that al-Awlaki was a traitor and a terrorist, there must be better rules of engagement than some "senior" bureaucrat making a decision to kill an American citizen without any accountability.

Elibiary condemned the convictions of the defendants in the Holy Land Foundation Trial as a loss for America and dismissed the prosecution as a political move. He is an expert in the practice of taqiyya, though one would doubt his lying prowess with the lame excuse he conjured when confronted with criticism over Khomeini. Though he at best sympathizes with Wahhabist style Islamists, he has been given a succession of sensitive advisory posts with: The Texas Department of Safety and National Counter-Terrorism Center Global Engagement Group; The Texas Department of Public Safety Advisory Board; and his most recent assignment with Homeland Security.

In 2011, Elibiary obtained security clearance which he immediately abused by accessing a classified intelligence sharing database. He reportedly wanted to leak materials to the press that could be misconstrued to portray presidential candidate Rick Perry of Texas as an Islamophobe.[83] In spite of his clear record, FBI Director Robert Mueller gave Elibiary the Louis E. Peters Memorial Award in September, 2011, for extraordinary contributions to specific cases; and expanded relationships with the Muslim-American Community in Texas.

Six days after Elibiary received his award, leftist radical Spencer Ackerman viciously attacked the FBI's Violent Extremism Training in a Wired magazine article. Elibiary has publicly expressed strong support for Ackerman. Shortly after this, Ackerman wrote another article commending Elibiary for his techniques with regard to Jihadists. A few days after that, Ackerman published another article further attacking the FBI. The article contained cell phone images within the FBI library at Quantico. The article attacked the FBI for having "islamophobic" materials in its library. Ironic that Ackerman had access to cell phone images right after Elibiary visited Quantico.

Mohamed Elibiary actively seeks to silence those who try to expose *Civilization Jihad* (see Chapter 2).[84]

Mohamed Magid

Huffington Post called Mohamed Magid America's Imam in 2011, but who is he? Magid is currently the President of Islamic Society of North America, ISNA. This organization is the largest Islamic umbrella group in the country. It was listed as a primary organization of the Muslim Brotherhood in their documents that were revealed during the Holy Land Foundation Trial. In fact, it was at the top of the list. ISNA was listed during that trial as an unindicted co-conspirator. ISNA is heavily involved in the propagation of Shari'a.

Magid was born and raised in Sudan where his father was the grand Mufti. He is Imam at the ADAMS Center (All Dulles Area Muslim Society) with its main campus in Sterling, VA. The ADAMS Center has seven branches serving over 5500 families. This mosque has been called one of the most dangerous mosques in the country, second only behind the late Anwar al Awlaki's Dar al-Hijrah mosque in Falls Church, VA.

As stated earlier, Al Awlaki was an al Qaeda leader who was targeted by the CIA and killed in a drone strike in Yemen in 2011. The Dar al-Hijrah mosque has tried to distance itself from the scrutiny brought on by its former leader's terrorist activity. It is claimed that al Awlaki's bent towards terror only happened after he left Dar al-Hijrah.[85]

Magid's Mosque is at the center of what has been called the Wahhabi Corridor. As its leader, Mohamed Magid projects himself as moderate but is in fact a Shari'a compliant Muslim Brother.[86] As will be documented in the next chapter, most moderates are not moderates at all.

In 2011, Magid was invited to the State Department to hear Obama's second Outreach to Muslims speech. He used that opportunity to lobby Secretary Timothy Geitner for the Brotherhood's bid to end impediments to *zakat*. Zakat is one of the five pillars of Islam. It requires Muslims to give of their means. It is further required that one-eighth of zakat must be allocated for Jihad. At President Obama's first Outreach to Muslims speech in Cairo in 2009, he said he was "committed to working with American Muslims to ensure that they can fulfill zakat."[87]

Remember, part of zakat must go to support Jihad, much of that money going to the venerated families of Jihadist martyrs. In helping zakat be fulfilled, President Obama is saying he will help assure that Jihad is supported.

Under Operation Green Quest in 2002, federal investigators alleged that over 100 different organizations, both non- profits and for-profit companies, were interconnected and suspected in the material support of terrorism, tax evasion and money laundering. This group has been known as the SAAR Network as well as the SAFA Group. The group was led by Muslim Brotherhood member, Jamal al Barzinijil, who had earlier founded the International Institute for Islamic Thought (IIIT). IIIT is another group listed by the Brotherhood as one of *its* organizations. The vice president of the group, Ahmed Totonji, was Chairman of the Board of Magid's Mosque complex, and he was also vice president of IIIT.

There are too many tentacles going in too many directions to discuss them all. Many of these organizations had offices at the same address in Herndon, Virginia. The feds raided the building in 2002. The ADAMS Center also had offices at that location. Magid was present when the raid took place. Interdepartmental turf war caused the investigation to be shut down in 2003. Although over 500 banker boxes of evidence were seized, no charges have ever come about.

Much of the money that finds its way to terrorist organizations comes through charitable outfits. The Sterling Charitable Gift Fund is one such organization that has been named in a government affidavit as having been involved in money laundering and the material support of terrorism. Magid was an adviser to this fund.[88]

Of Corruption, Deception and Outright Evil

Money laundering is a problem of gargantuan proportions. Organized Crime, Drug Cartels, and Terrorist organizations launder money through main line banks which continually look the other way. In the summer of 2012, global financial entity HSBC paid a $2 billion fine, which was a slap on the wrist for the banking giant.

U.S. law prohibits banks from doing business with what are considered dangerous countries or individuals. HSBC repeatedly ignored this and did business with Iran, Burma and North Korea.[89] They work their magic sending the dirty money out into their vast network, and abracadabra, it comes back as squeaky clean U.S. dollars. This is a little known, though immeasurably huge problem.

Poor anti-money laundering controls are, in our opinion, one of the biggest threats to our national security at this point in history. The terrorist organizations and criminal elements need money to do what they do. These criminally culpable banks are willingly greasing the wheels for those who would destroy us. Much more could be written on this, but it is a book in itself.[90] HBUS (HSBC-US) carried out 28,000 undisclosed sensitive transactions between 2001 and 2007. The vast majority of the nearly 20 billion dollars in transactions involved Iran. HBUS also provided services and U.S. dollars to terrorist linked Saudi banks.[91]

The Islamic Circle of North America (ICNA) set aside 3 million dollars in 2012 to promote Shari'a nation-wide.[92] Almost as soon as it was announced, Mohamed Magid lauded their efforts, but encouraged them to wash Shari'a from their vocabulary. He suggested they use words like, 'Muslim values' or 'Islamic values' to make Shari'a more palatable to non-Muslims.

ICNA also claims that efforts by states to disallow courts to consider Shari'a in making decisions are merely an attempt to "create a fear of Islam and Muslims in the larger society."[93] They completely ignore the *fact* that we already have laws that govern our states and our court systems. No group should be allowed to come in and use their own set of laws over and above ours. They see Shari'a as superior to the U.S. Constitution. ICNA was listed in the Muslim Brotherhood's Explanatory Memorandum as one of 29 like-minded organizations, with the same end in mind as the Brotherhood.

Muslim leaders like Magid have been enlisted by our government in advising agencies in all matters Islamic. Under Secretary Janet Napolitano, Magid was appointed to the Department of Homeland Security's Countering Violent Extremism Working Group, created to advise the Obama administration and intelligence agencies in what they *can* and *cannot* say. It is inexplicable why, Magid, the head of an organization named as an unindicted co-conspirator in a major terrorist financing case, is now advising the Obama administration what they are allowed to say about Islam.

Erasing the language of Jihad is top priority. Most trigger words have been eliminated over the past four years. For instance, the 2009 Fort Hood massacre by Major Nidal Malik Hasan, who screamed "Allah Akbar" while killing 13 people and wounded 29 others, was not labeled a terrorist attack, but rather "workplace violence."[94] People like Magid are affecting policy. The following is just one example of the changing language how any mention of Jihad or violence has been eliminated from key U.S. documents:[95]

	911 Commission Report 2004	FBI Counter-Terrorism Lexicon 2008
Violent Extremism	3	29
Enemy	39	0
Jihad	126	0
Muslim	145	0
Islam	322	0
Muslim Brotherhood	5	0
Religious	65	3
Hamas	4	0
Hezbollah	2	0
Al Qaeda	36	0
Caliph	7	0
Shari'a	2	0

The FBI chain of command at the Justice Department has made Magid, the ADAMS Center and ISNA central to its Muslim outreach efforts. Magid's connection goes all the way to the top of the DOJ to his meeting with Eric Holder.

At an event in October of 2011 at George Washington University, Assistant Attorney general Thomas Perez publicly embraced Magid, and at the same event, Deputy Attorney General James Cole said, "I recently directed all components of the Department of Justice to reevaluate their training efforts in a range of areas, from community outreach to national security."[96]

At that same time, U.S. Attorney Dwight Holton said, "I want to be perfectly clear about this. Training materials that portray Islam as a religion of violence or with a tendency towards violence are wrong. They are offensive and they are contrary to everything this President, this Attorney General, and Department of Justice stand for. They will not be tolerated."

FBI Director Mueller submitted to Islamist demands and purged files of "offensive" materials; 700 documents and 300 briefings were purged. But you give the proverbial inch...ISNA pushed for further meetings and the right to review future training materials, AND an open and transparent training process. At best, Attorney General Holder is violating U.S. law in meeting with those connected with unindicted co-conspirators.

It is as if these men have had their memories wiped, and blinders permanently implanted in their heads. The only other alternative is that the Obama administration is deliberately aiding and abetting individuals and organizations that are committed to overthrowing the U.S. government and our Constitution. Remember, radicals are no longer the fringe element of Islam. Islamists who hold these beliefs and will settle for nothing less than a global caliphate are taking over in country after country – most with U.S. approval and aid.

Education

The semantics police have hit in other areas as well. The Islamic takeover of education is well under way. Islamists, (mainly with Saudi money) have spent billions setting up departments for Islamic study at universities all over the country.

- $20 million to University of Arkansas
- $5 million to Berkeley from 2 Saudi Sheiks linked to al Qaeda
- $22.5 million to Harvard
- $28 million to Georgetown
- $11 million to Cornell
- $5 million to MIT
- $1.5 million to Texas A&M

- $5 million to Rutgers and Columbia, (who tried to conceal the source)
- More to UC Santa Barbara, John Hopkins, Syracuse, Howard, University of Chicago, USC, UCLA, Duke, and the list goes on.[97]

The Saudis have also spent vast amounts of money developing, marketing and placing K-12 curriculum into U.S. public schools. Again, this would be a book in itself. We will just look at one text book, *History Alive, The Medieval World and Beyond*, published by Teacher's Curriculum Institute in Palo Alto, CA. The textbook has over 40 pages devoted to Muhammad and Islam, with more pages not in the book but available in the form of photos and maps that the teachers can share with students. Catholicism gets a mere 10 pages.

When the curriculum was first put into use in one small school on the East Coast, the educators were in shock at the redefining of terms they were finding. One such term was "Jihad." The curriculum claimed that it merely meant "the struggle." The teaching focuses on the inner spiritual striving for devotion to faith. That is what the text writers are teaching the next generation of children. The curriculum completely ignores the much more accurate definition of Jihad, which is an external struggle against the enemies of Islam, which by definition is *anyone* who is not a Muslim. This is another example of taqiyya – lying or deceiving for the faith – which will be discussed in detail in chapter six.

Students who read this text book will be taught all about the life of Muhammad from a decidedly pro-Islamic perspective and they are promised they will, "learn more about the holy book called the Qur'an. Together with Sunnah—the example of Muhammad..." The text book teaches the kids that most Muslims reject violence and that "non-Muslims under Muslim rule were usually allowed to practice their faiths." They must have forgotten the Armenian Holocaust that took 3 million lives and the thousands even now who are imprisoned and killed in multiple countries simply for rejecting Islam.

On page 88 of the textbook, students are told that Islam, Judaism, and Christianity have much in common. And that "Muslims believe that all three religions worship the same God." That too is taqiyya, as will be explained in Chapter 6. If it can happen in this school, it can happen in your school.

Attack and Destroy

Many other Islamic organizations are wielding influence as well. More than this book can contain. They are affecting policy at every level. If anyone dares to speak out against these organizations or individuals, they are immediately attacked. Congresswoman, Michelle Bachman expressed concerns over Huma Abedin's Muslim Brotherhood connections and many of the connections cited earlier in Chapter 4. She was immediately attacked by numerous progressive liberals as well as every mainline media outlet. The People for the American Way (PFAW) led the attack. The PFAW is a far-left progressive liberal nongovernmental organization partially funded by George Soros.

Bachmann's crime? According to Michael Keegan, president of PFAW:

"Michele Bachmann has used her position on the Intelligence Committee to spread conspiracy theories and smear the reputations of honorable public servants. Speaker Boehner himself called her actions 'dangerous.' It's mysterious, then, why he [Boehner] has chosen to reward her reckless extremism with continued access to sensitive national security information and a powerful platform for her agenda."[98]

Baseless? Conspiracy theories? Smear tactics? Extremism? The only one guilty of these charges is Keegan and others like him. It is called "projection;" projecting onto others what you are guilty of yourself. It is done not only to vilify the opposition, but to shift scrutiny away from the accuser. It is a very common tool used by progressive liberals (and Islamists) to attack and smear anyone who would point out their own progressive faults and lies.

In Bachmann's case, there are numerous independent sources detailing all the interconnections of organizations and people Bachmann revealed.[99] Some of them are cited above in this chapter. In fact, Bachmann is one of the very few who is trying to sound the alarm of the extreme danger of Islamic penetration of our government. Most progressive Republicans have attacked her as well.

Perhaps the greatest vindication of Bachmann and others who are investigating Islamic influence in the U.S. government comes from Egypt's Rose El-Youssef magazine.

"Perhaps the most famous story the American media dealt with months ago was 'Huma Abidin' Clinton's special adviser and her close friend, but what many people do not know is that there are 6 other personalities tied to the Brotherhood on the American political street... Are these six personalities tantamount to a turning point for the Obama administration from a position hostile to Islamic groups and organizations in the world to the largest and most important supporter of the Muslim Brotherhood in the world...?"[100]

The author of the Rose El-Youssef magazine's article, Ahmed Shawki, was very supportive of having Islamists in the Obama administration. He reaffirms Bachmann's accusations and mentions many more. Was he exaggerating, looking for "street creds?" Or, more likely, he was merely restating what many other investigators, including Bachmann have found.

The worst connection may be Obama himself.

5 - The Obama Connection

"...we will have a Muslim in the White House in 2008"
Radio broadcast from Saudi Arabia pre 2008

The Islamic connections get worse. Avi Lipkin, a well-known author of *Is Fanatic Islam a Global Threat?*, was one of the first people to raise the alarm of Islamic fanaticism in 1995. Well before 2008, he and his wife Rachel reported radio broadcasts from Saudi Arabia that were claiming "we will have a Muslim in the White House in 2008."[101] Avi Lipkin was born in Flushing, New York, but immigrated to Israel at age 19. Before leaving, he majored in Sovietology at New York University, then Spanish/Latin American Studies at Hebrew University, graduating in 1973.

He served in the IDF actively in 1973 and as a reservist until 1989 when he became an officer in the IDF Spokesman's Office until 2001. During that time he worked as a senior editor and translator in the News Department of the Government Press Office as part of Prime Minister Yitzhak Shamir's Office at Beit Agron. He has authored numerous books, been interviewed on hundreds of radio and TV shows and has spoken to hundreds of audiences worldwide.

Rachel Lipkin is an Egyptian born Jew who speaks fluent Arabic. Immigrating to Israel in 1969, she has worked for Israel's Radio Service in Arabic for the past 25 years monitoring Arabic language broadcasts on radio and TV as well as newspapers.

On January 19, 2010, Rachel recorded a broadcast from Nile TV out of Egypt. It was a roundtable discussion wherein Egypt's foreign minister reportedly said that he had a one-on-one meeting with Obama who swore to him that he is a Muslim. Obama then explained to him about all his Muslim family background and practices. Obama then said "I have a problem with some domestic issues, and as soon as I finish with the health care question you Muslims will see what I will do for Islam regarding Israel."[102]

There is little doubt the quotes above were really said over the airwaves. However, caution is advised. As stated in Chapter 1, page 7, Islam uses deception, or taqiyya (obligatory lying for the faith) to achieve their goals.[103] These radio and TV proclamations could be deliberate deceptions. However, it is interesting, and perhaps telling, that Obama has shunned Israel, and on May 5, 2011 shocked the world by calling for Israel to withdraw back to its pre-1967 borders. Doing so would make Israel indefensible. Obama knew that when he said it.[104]

The Inexplicable Explained?

If all this is true, it would give new meaning to the deep bow Obama gave to the King of Saudi Arabia in 2009 during his global apology trip that shocked Americans. It would also explain the mystery of how Obama, coming from a low-income family, could comfortably attend so many prestigious and very expensive universities. It might even explain why Obama kept trying to force the bizarre narrative that the September 11, 2012 Benghazi attack on the U.S. Mission was precipitated by the anti-Muhammad video rather than Islamists.

Clare Lopez, former CIA officer and currently Senior Fellow at the Center for Security Policy as well as the Clarion Fund determined:

> The Obama administration, and especially the Department of State led by Secretary of State Hillary Clinton, are coordinating closely with the OIC [Organization of the Islamic Conference] to achieve implementation of U.N. Human Rights Commission Resolution 16/18 [see discussion on page 15], which despite some cosmetic wording changes, remains the vehicle through which the OIC is determined to work toward the criminalization of the criticism of Islam in U.S. law.[105]

Lopez also found that the Obama administration's "stubborn adherence to the false narrative of the YouTube film, 'Innocence of Muslims,' for so long after the September 11, 2012 attack on the

Benghazi mission is inexplicable except in the context of a globally coordinated campaign through the OIC and U.S. Muslim Brotherhood affiliates to advance the anti-free speech agenda of U.N. Resolution 16/18." She claims the administration is attempting to "move Middle East policy in a direction that favors Jihadist states."[106]

Again, if true, it would explain why Secretary of State Clinton used a series of convoluted excuses not to tell the American people her role in the Benghazi mission and CIA annex tragedy. She refused to go on the Sunday news shows on September 16, five days after the 9/11 Benghazi tragedy to explain what happened at Benghazi. Instead, UN Ambassador Susan Rice, with full knowledge of the facts known by the administration, was sent to push the false narrative (perhaps unknowingly) that it was the YouTube video that sparked the attack.

After four months and numerous postponements, Clinton finally gave testimony to the Senate on January 23, 2013. When asked about the blunders and the continued narrative that it was the video that caused it, Clinton responded with arms flailing and voice at high pitch, "The fact is we had four dead Americans. Was it because of a protest or was it because of guys out for a walk one night and decided they'd go kill some Americans? What difference at this point does it make?"[107]

What difference does it make? People died, including Ambassador Stevens followed by a massive cover-up. Clinton's statement wasn't intended to explain anything. Her bizarre answer was intended to intimidate the Senate committee from asking any more penetrating questions. It worked. She side-stepped every poorly worded question that could have revealed the truth of what actually happened before, during and after the Benghazi attack. She never even called it terrorism.

Clinton even claimed that she never got the correspondence from Ambassador Stevens that security in Benghazi was desperately lacking and could not repel the kind of attack that eventually killed him. It's hard to imagine that mid-level bureaucrats would not have brought these pleas for help to her attention.

As bad as this is, there may be a more sinister reason for the constantly changing and unbelievably bizarre storyline the Obama administration kept trying to feed the American people for weeks. Put aside the fact that Obama immediately knew the attack was by terrorists and not a video. Within a week of the September 11, 2012 Benghazi attack, stories began to trickle out that Ambassador Stevens, at the direction of Obama and Clinton, was coordinating a clandestine operation to provide Jihadi fighters and guns out of Benghazi, through Turkey, to Syrian rebels. Some of these Jihadists were al Qaeda fighters.[108]

Researcher and *The New York Times* bestselling author Aaron Klein was tracking this connection even before the September 11, 2012 Benghazi attacks, which was adamantly denied by the White House and State Department officials.[109] "Stevens," Klein determined, "played a central role in recruiting Jihadists to fight Bashar Assad's regime in Syria, according to Egyptian security officials." Many of the rebels in both Libya and Syria were members of al Qaeda, "many of whom had fought U.S. troops in Iraq and Afghanistan."[110]

Clinton had good reason to hide. The unclassified report from a Special Accountability Review Board on the Benghazi Attack damned the State Department by laying the blame squarely on "leadership… deficiencies…at senior levels" that left the security at the Benghazi Special Mission "grossly inadequate to deal with the attack that took place."[111] That leadership certainly includes Clinton.

The stench of Benghazi is orders of magnitude worse than the Nixon Watergate Scandal and Bush Valerie Plame Scandal (CIA Leak Scandal) combined. The press coverage on these two scandals was relentless, droning on month after month. Conversely, the mainstream media yawned at Benghazi; at most delegating two or three paragraphs on page 6, or a thirty second mention on the evening news.

The nomination of John Brennan to head the CIA and Chuck Hagel as Secretary of Defense fits perfectly in Obama's apparent rush to embrace Islam. As station chief in the 1990s for the CIA in Saudi Arabia, Brennan is reported to have converted to Islam with several U.S. officials in his presence. After former FBI Counterterrorism Agent John Guandolo interviewed these unnamed witnesses, he believed the conversion was a Saudi counterintelligence operation designed to "turn" Brennan into an Islamist asset.[112]

While converting to Islam does not make Brennan a direct threat to the United States, if he was turned to Islam in order to accept the Islamic doctrine of a global caliphate, the threat becomes quite real. It would be like promoting a former CIA station chief for Moscow to CIA Director after he was actively converted to communism while serving in Moscow. Like Islam, communism has a goal of subverting the U.S. on the way to world domination. Yet, to our knowledge, no inquiry has ever been made into Brennan's "conversion," or even if it really occurred. Apparently, the White House deems it unimportant.

Guandolo claims in his webpage's "about" section that he "created and implemented the FBI's first *Counterterrorism Training/ Education Program* in 2006, focusing on the Muslim Brotherhood and their subversive movement in the United States, Islamic Doctrine, and the global Islamic Movement."[113] That seems to make him an expert on the subject.

However, Guandolo's voracity is often attacked by critics because he was forced to resign from the FBI after a list was uncovered enumerating his sexual conquests of other agents while he was on the job, and while he was a married man.[114] In fairness, while his behavior was immoral and inexcusable, critics accusing Guandolo had no problem with former U.S. presidents staying in office after similar exploits were revealed.

What concerned Guandolo was that Brennan:

"has interwoven his life professionally and personally with individuals that we know are terrorists, and he has given them access to not only senior leaders inside the government, but has given them access to the National Security Council, the national security staff. He has brought known Hamas and Muslim Brotherhood operatives into those positions of government. He has overseen and approved and encouraged others to bring *known leaders of Hamas and the Muslim Brotherhood into the government in positions to advise the US Government on counterterrorism strategy as well as the overall...'War on Terror.'"* (Emphasis added) [115]

Like Obama, Brennan glowingly praises Islam. In an interview on the Tom Trento radio show on February 10, 2013, Guandolo asserted that Brennan is clueless and grossly ignorant of the goals and strategies of al Qaeda. Even though he recognizes al Qaeda is the enemy, Brennan claims to believe that al Qaeda is the *only* enemy. Apparently, the

Muslim Brotherhood is fine because they believe in "...peace and tolerance..."[116] Brennan even publically calls Jerusalem "Al-Quds," its Islamic name.[117]

Like Brennan, Secretary of Defense Chuck Hagel's background is also problematic. In June 2001 and March 2002 Hagel addressed conferences sponsored by Iranian-backed American-Iranian Council in Washington. The conferences emphasized the need to stop sanctions against Iran and open trade with the terrorist-sponsoring nation. Hagel also opposed numerous bills and resolutions in 2006 and 2008 that would have increased pressure on Iran to abandon its broad support of terrorism. Rather than sanctions, Hagel favored a policy of outreach, negotiation, and accommodation with Iran.[118] As will be explained in Chapters 6 and 7, this approach has, and will never, work.

Hagel is also reported to have said that the U.S. Department of State was an extension of the Israeli government in a 2007 speech at Rutgers.[119] It was not surprising that Iran publically endorsed Hagel's appointment as Secretary of Defense.

While all of this is somewhat circumstantial, Lopez states that it is consistent with Obama's embracing of Islam: "The White House cultivates relationships with CAIR, Hamas, the Muslim Brotherhood leadership and associates," while "instructors, trainers and any curriculum that would describe accurately the link between Islamic doctrine, law and scripture and Islamic terrorism have been methodically purged from U.S. government, intelligence and law enforcement classrooms."[120]

Daniel Pipes, president of the Middle East Forum, attempted to make sense out of all the conflicting information about Obama's background:

> ...Available evidence suggests that Obama was born and raised a Muslim and retained a Muslim identity until his late 20s. Child to a line of Muslim males, given a Muslim name, registered as a Muslim in two Indonesian schools, he read the Qur'an in religion class, still recites the Islamic declaration of faith and speaks to Muslim audiences like a fellow believer. Between his non-practicing Muslim father, his Muslim stepfather and his

four years of living in a Muslim milieu, he was seen by others and saw himself as a Muslim.

This is not to say that he was a practicing Muslim or that he remains a Muslim today — much less an Islamist... The issue is that Mr. Obama has specifically and repeatedly lied about his Muslim identity. More than any other single deception, Mr. Obama's treatment of his own religious background exposes his moral failings.[121]

The Islamist Obamas in Kenya

It is a matter of record that President Obama's family, his close family in Africa, is devoutly Muslim. That they further adhere to an austere form of Islam doesn't play well in Peoria so the media is silent.

After the election of Barack Obama to the presidency of the United States, the Obamas of Kogelo were catapulted to exponentially heightened status; rags to riches overnight. In an interview on Al Jazeera the president's first cousin proudly revealed that he studied Arabic and Shari'a in Saudi Arabia in Medina.[122] As stated before, only one brand of Islam is taught at that Islamic University; Salafist, aka, Wahhabi Islam.

The Kenyan Obamas' power and influence both in Kenya and internationally has given them the ability to pursue significant advancement of Wahhabi Islam. In 2009, Barack Obama's uncle, Sayid Obama, his grandmother, Sarah Omar, and cousin, Musa Ismail Obama, made their pilgrimage to Mecca. They were received by members of the Saudi royal family including Prince Faisal bin Thamer bin Abdul Aziz, Prince Abdul Aziz Bin Mamdouh Bin Abdul Aziz, and Prince Abdullah bin Nayef bin Abdul Aziz, as well as a number of other princes and officials. The Saudis provided extensive security for the President's family while they were in Saudi Arabia.

Musa Obama gave his interview on Al Jazeera TV after the trip.[123] During that interview, Musa discussed his own devotion to Islam as well as that of his family. He talked about how it had been a lifelong dream of his grandmother (she is also President Obama's grandmother) to perform Hajj. Hajj is one of the 5 pillars of Islam and is the ultimate act of worship for the Muslim. Musa said that his grandmother,

Sarah, had believed that it would never be a reality for her to perform Hajj by making the trek to Mecca and that she was deeply moved that she was able to do so.

Musa is very proud of the fact that he has memorized the Qur'an and studied Arabic and Shari'a in Saudi Arabia at the Islamic University in Medina.[124] This university is nothing but a channel for the proliferation of Wahhabist beliefs. He stated during the Al Jazeera interview that he had to travel 700 miles away from home in his village of Kogelo in Western Kenya in order to study the Qur'an. He laments the fact that Western Kenya has no Islamic centers for this kind of study.

Musa wants to see Wahhabi education in the school systems of Kenya in the same way as it is taught in the schools in Saudi Arabia. During the interview, Musa also bemoaned the fact that proselytizing for Islam in Kenya has been very difficult because of the influence of Christianity. President Obama's cousin was very careful during the interview not to allow questions that might be politically damaging for the president.[125]

During the interview, Musa also talked about his family's charitable organization started by his grandmother, the Sarah Obama Benevolent Fund Institute. The purported function of this organization is to help orphans and widows, those suffering from HIV/AIDS, as well as offering aid to students by providing scholarships to university. The Al Jazeera interview revealed that the majority of the funds raised go to send students to the Wahhabist educational institutions in Saudi Arabia.

Musa also stated that the organization is helping orphans, though they are only aiding a mere 50 orphans and 150 widows. At the same time, they are sending so many students, a "flood," to the radical Islamic University in Medina, that Musa and Sayid had to meet with the head of another Wahhabist university, Umm Al-Qura University in Mecca, to start sending students there as well because the university in Medina didn't have enough slots for all the students they were sending.

President Obama's uncle Sayid Obama is very active in his work with the Muslim World League, which has numerous connections with terrorist groups including al Qaeda.[126] They provided sponsorship as well as material support to Osama bin Laden. According to President

Obama's cousin Musa, the president is in continual contact with the Kenyan branch of his family through regular phone calls to his favorite uncle, Sayid. The Kenyan branch of the Obama family uses funds raised through Sarah Omar's charitable organization to propagate this radical form of Islam.[127]

The penetration of Islam into the federal government is astonishing and alarming. The potential direct link of the Obama clan, and possibly Obama himself, to Wahhabi Islam has staggering implications for the very future of the United States of America.

In spite of this readily accessible information, not one word of this has been brought up in the mainstream press over the past four years. It is very doubtful Obama would have been elected the first time, let alone the second, if the American people knew of his potential extreme Islamist connections.

Obama has spent millions of dollars preventing anyone from uncovering his very secret and increasingly alarming Marxist, and now Islamist past. While proclaiming in 2008 and again in 2013 he is the most transparent president in the history of America, he has been just the opposite. Even the far left media is finally becoming alarmed. Leftist *Politico* wrote this scathing attack on Obama on February 18, 2013:

"President Barack Obama is a master at limiting, shaping and manipulating media coverage of himself and his White House. ... The mastery mostly flows from a White House that has taken old tricks for shaping coverage (staged leaks, friendly interviews) and put them on steroids using new ones (social media, content creation, precision targeting)... The balance of power between the White House and press has tipped unmistakably toward the government. This is an arguably dangerous development, and one that the Obama White House ... has exploited cleverly and ruthlessly."[128]

Obama's strategy of deception has worked beautifully. The majority of Americans voted for him—twice! They continue to support him as he "fundamentally transforms America."

Obama's Fundamental Transformation of America

The following is a short list of just some of the extremism of Obama in fulfilling his promise that he would "fundamentally transform" America:

- He has intentionally demeaned the Prime Minister of Israel, our greatest ally in the Mid- East with the Washington Post saying that Netanyahu was treated like an "unsavory third world dictator."
- The President employed al Qaradawi, key spiritual advisor to the Muslim Brotherhood, as an intermediary with the Taliban.
- He turned NASA into an organization for Muslim Outreach.
- President Obama bowed to the Saudi King, even though the White House press secretary said it was just an illusion that occurred because of the difference in the height of the two men.
- He gave 1.5 billion dollars to the Muslim Brotherhood dominated and led government of Egypt and sold them F16's which will likely be used against Israel.
- In one of the most outrageous, revealing moves by Obama, he demands that Israel go back to its indefensible pre-1967 borders.
- He is supporting efforts to insert Islamic doctrine into our public education, including how to become a Muslim, while minimizing (some say attacking) Christianity on every front.
- He is taking a "kid gloves" approach to Iran's nuclear program and violations of human rights with no change in policy in sight (like engaging with Congress as per the Constitution)
- He allowed the Benghazi U.S. Consulate's ability to defend itself deteriorate in spite of pleas from the ambassador to beef up defenses; did nothing to help the consulate and CIA facility once under attack (in fact, did not even talk to Defense Secretary Leon Panetta during the attack),[129] and then tried to blame a ridiculous internet video for the attack rather than al Qaeda, who he claimed to have already defeated after it was well known to be al Qaeda, not the video that caused the attack. Then he lied about everything with a straight face and indignation. Four Americans died; one of them Ambassador Stevens.

- Obama's Attorney General's office (DOJ) has not prosecuted any black on white racial violence, yet vigorously prosecutes white on black violence.
- He used the tragedy at Sandy Hook Elementary to push a political gun agenda, by signing 23 executive orders further eroding the Second Amendment.
- He repeatedly funnels loan money to those that have supported him financially in his campaigns (like Solyndra and GM) while attacking those that do not support him (like Fox News even though Fox is owned by Rupert Murdoch).
- He added $5.5 trillion to our national debt his first four years and refuses to take action to reduce the $122 trillion unfunded entitlement liability.
- His economic policies are literally destroying the middle class in general and the U.S. economy in particular.
- He is changing U.S. policy through executive orders bypassing Congress' Constitutionally divided powers.
- He is socializing and Islamizing America right before our eyes.

With nation after nation falling to Shari'a control as the Arab Spring turns into the Arab winter, and now with everything we are learning about our own president, the time has come to wake up and take action. We need intelligence officers who truly have our national security as top priority. Not ones who say things like James Clapper did before the House Intelligence Committee, where he claimed that with regard to the Islamists, there is no "overarching agenda, particularly in pursuit of violence, at least internationally."

Taken all together, the Obama administration is either woefully ignorant of the Islamic endgame, or they are deliberately allowing our government to be compromised with Islamist doctrine. Maybe if Obama, Clinton, Clapper, Hagel and Brennan watched the Free Syrian Army carving heads off with pocket knives; or did not view the horrific events in Egypt, Tunisia, Yemen, Libya, through rose colored glasses, they would not be so supportive of Islam.

We also need an Attorney General who won't neuter the FBI and render the DOJ Shari'a compliant. We don't need a Secretary of State who lies when an ambassador is killed, and who doesn't jump on board with the Islamists at the UN who want to crush our First Amendment with Shari'a compliant blasphemy laws, and who doesn't clear the way for a Hamas funding, grandson of Hassan al-Banna to gain entry to the U.S. Fortunately, Hillary Clinton has retired, but will probably run for president in 2016. Will now Secretary of State John Kerry be any better?

Finally, we need a president who actually likes America. Remember what the Islamists have said. All we have to do is listen to what they say:

- Mahmoud Ahmadinejad: "This movement is certainly on its rightful path of creation, ensuring a promising future for humanity. A future that will be built when humanity initiates to trend the path of the divine prophets and the righteous under the leadership of Imam al-Mahdi..."[130]
- Muhammad Morsi urged Egyptians to "nurse our children and our grandchildren on hatred" for Jews and Zionists. In a television interview, he described Zionists as "these bloodsuckers who attack the Palestinians, these warmongers, the descendants of apes and pigs"[131]
- Recep Tayyip Erdogan, Prime Minister of Turkey who is helping ensure ultimate Muslim Brotherhood dominance in Syria, "The mosques are our barracks, the domes our helmets, the minarets our bayonets and the faithful our soldiers..."[132]

6 – Real-World Biblical Implications

"...Allah also conspired, for He is the greatest of all deceivers." *Qur'an 3:54*

Perhaps, you, the reader, are offended by dragging religion, especially the Bible and Christianity into any discussion. In this case it is unavoidable. It is imperative that you understand that almost everything we are experiencing now has spiritual roots that you need to understand. You can slam this book closed if you want, but by doing so you *will* leave yourself wide open to deception.

By now, readers should be surprised, if not shocked, about how much misinformation about Islam the Western World has been force-fed. Islam is not a religion of peace, as we constantly read or hear in the news media. True, many Muslims want to peacefully live with us Kaffir's, or unbelievers. However, as Walid Shoebat (the former Palestinian terrorist) and Joel Richardson explain in their exhaustive book, *God's War on Terror*, only a small minority of Muslims truly believe in peace. Even most so-called Muslim moderates, so extolled by the press and political leaders, are moderates in name only.

The truly moderate Muslims are called "liberals" and eventually will be treated as if they were Kaffir's themselves – only slightly better than dogs because they betrayed the Qur'an. Actually, when the root word for Kaffir (also Kafir, Kufr and Kuffar) is understood, it becomes very clear what standing a Kaffir has in Islam. In the Qur'an a Kaffir is referred to as:

- Mocked: "But on this Day the Believers will laugh at the Unbelievers." [83:34]

- Punished: "But ye have indeed rejected (Him), and soon will come the inevitable (punishment)!" [25:77]
- Terrorized: "I will instill terror into the hearts of the Unbelievers." [8:12]
- Destroyed: "Of the wrong-doers the last remnant was cut off. Praise be to God, the Cherisher of the Worlds." [6:45]
- Slain: "Seize them and slay them wherever ye get them: in their case we have provided you with a clear argument against them." [4:91]
- Crucified: "The punishment of those who wage war against God [Allah] and His Apostle [Mohammed], and strive with might and main for mischief through the land is: execution, or crucifixion, or the cutting off of hands and feet from opposite sides." [5:33]
- Evil: "Say thou: 'Yea, and ye shall then be humiliated (on account of your evil)." [37:8]
- Cursed: "They shall have a curse on them: wherever they are found." [33:61][133]

In other words, once Islam dominates a country, a Kaffir's life becomes worthless, and his life expectancy very short. The hoax about Islam being a religion of peace and harmony that has merely been hijacked is a lie out of the pit of hell. There is a reason for this. The real beliefs of Islam literally leap off the pages of the Bible.

In some ways, Walid Shoebat's life story is not uncommon for Muslims who have rejected Islam. He was born and raised in, of all places, Bethlehem, the birthplace of Jesus. But that meant nothing. He was a rabid terrorist who, although he had never actually killed anyone (but came close), he *hated* all Jews and Christianity with a passion. Even though his mother was a Christian, he was deeply committed to radical Islam and knew the Qur'an backward and forward. Then the unforeseeable happened. He fell in love with a Christian Catholic.

Such a thing was not uncommon, and in most cases the Islamist husband lies to his girlfriend, fiancée, and finally his wife about his real Islamic beliefs. That is what Walid planned on doing. He lied to his fiancé and her mother. He told the mother he believes in Jesus, whom all Muslims do; just not that Jesus is the Son of God.[134] As discussed in Chapters 1, 4 and 5, that is perfectly all right under the practice of taqiyya (lying for the faith).

Many Western women who marry Muslim men have found out the hard way that they were deceived; often after going to the husband's homeland on vacation, only to find they are never permitted to return home. This is exactly what had happened to Walid's mother. Although this is what Walid thought he would do, that was not to be his fate. His wife explained some things about the Bible that intrigued Walid, and she challenged him to disprove it. He decided (like other Muslims and agnostics alike) to investigate so as to prove the Bible was corrupt – just as he was taught.

Walid was stunned; "I kept asking myself, how did the Bible perfectly predict all of our plans to destroy Israel thousands of years ago in advance? Why was Jehovah defending Israel in the Bible? Why was it that whatever Allah loved, Jehovah hated, and whatever Jehovah loved, Allah hated? Allah hated the Jews. Jehovah loved them."[135]

As Walid continued reading his shock deepened; "You can't imagine how I felt when I read the Bible and found so much that describes the Mahdi who I learned so much about growing up. The shock to me was that, while a character identical to my Mahdi was seen throughout the pages of the Bible, this character was not called "the Mahdi," but rather, what Christians today call "the Antichrist."[136]

The Mahdi vs. Jesus
The Mahdi

Once, when Walid Shoebat was speaking with James Woolsey, the former director of the CIA (Central Intelligence Agency), Woolsey expressed his admiration of Sheikh Hisham Kabbani, saying he was his favorite "moderate" Muslim because Kabbani openly fought terrorism.[137] Remember, however, there is one basic Islamic ideology and two schools of thought within all the sects of Islam that seeks Global domination. One believes in terrorism and violence to conquer the world (like al Qaida, Hamas, Hezbollah and probably Iran) and the other believes in slow but effective penetration of the culture and government until the final stage when violence will be necessary (like

Wahhabis and the Muslim Brotherhood). The goal is the same for both; a global caliphate.

Walid explained to Woolsey that Kabbani is a "devout believer in the coming of the Mahdi. He is awaiting the Mahdi to come and establish Sharia law not only in America but the entire world."[138] This is a major foundational belief of nearly every Muslim, regardless of the specific sect to which they belong.

Almost all Muslims expect the Mahdi to return at any time to create a global caliphate. Kabbani, chairman of the Islamic Supreme Council of America and "moderate" friend of former CIA chief James Woolsey confirmed, "The coming of the Mahdi is an established doctrine for both Sunni and Shi'a Muslims, and indeed for all humanity."[139]

Most Shi'ite Muslims believe the Mahdi is Muhammad al-Mahdi, the twelfth Imam returned from the Occultation, where he has been hidden by God since 874. These Muslims are called Twelvers. The Occultation refers to a belief that the messianic Mahdi, who Shi'tes thought is an infallible male descendant of Mohammed, was born but disappeared, and will one day return and fill the world with justice.

As noted in Chapter 1, Iranian President Mahmoud Ahmadinejad expects the Mahdi's return in his lifetime. Ahmadinejad prayed in the 2005 UN General Assembly meeting, "O mighty Lord, I pray to you to hasten the emergence of your last repository, the promised one, that perfect and pure human being, the one that will fill this world with justice and peace." He might as well have added that the justice and peace he prays for will come *only* if the world proclaims the "Shahadatan:" "There is no God but Allah, and Mohammed is His messenger." Any person or nation who makes this statement has instant peace; as long as they back it up with Jihad.

Ironically, even though Muslims claim that Allah is the only god, Mohammed means "The Praised One" in Arabic. Muslim scholars go out of their way to assign to Mohammed titles that only belong to god. In pure hypocrisy, Qur'an 33:56 states "Allah and His angels pray upon the prophet. O ye who believe pray upon him and salute him with a worthy salutation." If Mohammed is not a deity, why are Allah and Muslims required to pray to him?[140]

In a similar fashion, Qur'an 45:12 Mohammed is the center of praise both in heaven and on the earth: "He (Allah) has subjected to you (Mohammed) whatever is in the heavens and whatever is in the earth." Finally, whenever you read Muslim literature in English you will see the PBUH – Peace Be Upon Him. The Arabic phrase for this is Salla Allâhû `A´layhi wa sallam, which more correctly means "the prayers and salutation of Allah be upon him (Mohammed). Ibn Katheer, the classical Qur'an commentator notes that Salla by itself is used to refer to "bowing and prostration."[141] How can Allah (god) be bowing to Mohammed, his supposed prophet and servant?

Sunni's, including Wahhabi's generally believe that the Mahdi will merely be of Mohammad's lineage, without specific reference to an individual. Abu Sa`id al-Khudri (a younger companion of Mohammed and prolific writer in the Hadith[d]) said in the Hadith (the sacred writings of Islam), "The Messenger of God (Mohammed) said: "The Mahdi is of my lineage, with a high forehead and a long, thin, curved nose. He will fill the earth with fairness and justice as it was filled with oppression and injustice, and he will rule for seven years."[142] Although a few other scholars suggest other time periods, they are the exception. Walid Shoebat is convinced that this is the same seven year tribulation period prophesied in the Bible when Jesus returns.

If the world does not proclaim the "Shahadatan," when, and if, the Mahdi returns, there will be war, death and forced submission. Iranian and Mideast analysts strongly believe that is the ***primary*** reason for Iran's development of a nuclear bomb. However, the war/violence option is not restricted to Iran. Understand that while there are exceptions, this belief runs strong in *most* Muslims who accept "the Qur'an as the word of Allah and the Mahdi as their "savior;" even so-called "moderate" Muslims.

Walid Shoebat provides an example of a time when he and a Messianic Jew rabbi (a Jewish Christian) were taken to lunch by a pastor to a restaurant across the street from the pastor's church. The pastor ate there on a regular basis and commented that he had never been treated badly. When the waiter came Walid told him in Arabic,"Assalamu Alakum" (peace be upon you).

---

[d] *Hadith* a narrative record of the sayings or customs of Muhammad and his companions. Also, the collective body of traditions relating to Muhammad and his companions.

The waiter responded, "Wa-Alaykum Assalam Warahmatullahi Wabarakatuh (and peace be upon you, Allah's mercy and His blessings.)

The exchange identified Walid as a Muslim and that he could be trusted. After a few laughs, Walid said,

"Do you believe this; I am sitting here with a Christian pastor and a rabbi?"

Walid then quoted an Islamic end-time prophecy that the trees and stones (see page 24) will cry out for Muslims to kill Jews. Continuing, Walid said,

"So what do you think? Is it valid to kill Jews?" asked Walid

"No," the waiter replied, "the time is not right. We need to wait for the Mahdi!"

The waiter was using classic taqiyya (obligatory lying or deceiving for the faith). He was biding his time until the Mahdi appeared. The very Kaffirs he was serving he would then be allowed to kill. Taqiyya is used by nearly all Muslims on a daily basis. It not only highlights the basic belief in the coming of the Mahdi, even with moderates, but also the fundamental fact you cannot trust any Muslim at face value. Certainly, there are Muslims who do not believe in the Mahdi, Shiri'a law or violence. Perhaps there are even a significant percentage of them.

The huge ongoing riots in Egypt in early 2013 against the long-anticipated tyranny of President Morsi and the Muslim Brotherhood certainly suggest that a significant number of the Egyptian Muslim population doesn't want Shari'a law. But how can you tell them apart from the majority who do believe in the Mahdi and violence? The truth is you can't. Remember those "Muslims" who don't believe in the Mahdi, Shiri'a law and violence are considered Kaffir, and will meet the same fate as you and I; if (when) the Mahdi "comes."

Jesus

The Qur'an (5:73) denies the Christian Trinity that Jesus is God, "They blaspheme who say that Allah is the third of three." In contrast, Genesis 1:24 states, "Then God said, "Let *us* make mankind in our image, in *our* likeness..." This is plural. Elsewhere God says he is "one God" so there aren't three Gods, there is one God of three parts, Father, Son and Holy Spirit.

One of the most amazing dialogues of Jesus's deity occurs in John 8 when the Pharisees try to prove Jesus was a fraud and a heretic so they could stone him. In verse 54 Jesus states, "My father, whom you claim as your God..." Jesus claims he is the Son of God. In verse 56 Jesus claims that Abraham saw Jesus in his day. To that the Pharisees exclaimed in verse 57, "You are not yet fifty years old...and you [say that you] have seen Abraham!" To this Jesus answered in verse 58, "Very truly I tell you," Jesus answered, "before Abraham was born, I am!"

Jesus' answer is perhaps the most astonishing of the Biblical proofs of his deity. He was saying that he, Jesus, was the "I am" in Exodus 3:14. Jesus was referring to when Moses was standing before the burning bush and asked God whom he should tell the Israelites had spoken to him. God answered, "I AM WHO I AM. This is what you are to say to the Israelites: 'I AM has sent me to you.'" Jesus made many claims that he was the Son of God. Either he was the greatest liar and deceiver of all time, or he was telling the truth. *There is no other choice.*

The Qur'an and Hadith don't directly call Jesus a liar, but do say the Bible has been corrupted and that the claim to deity is blasphemy. In verse 5:17, the Qur'an states, "In blasphemy indeed are those that say that God is Christ the son of Mary." Qur'an 4:157-158 affirms this: "That they [Kaffirs] said, 'We killed Christ Jesus and the son of Mary, the Messenger of Allah;' but they killed him not, nor crucified him, but so it was made to appear to them [Kaffirs], and those who differ therein are full of doubts, with no knowledge, but only conjecture to follow, for of a surety they killed him not: Nay, Allah raised him [Jesus] up to Himself [Allah]; and Allah is Exalted in Power, Wise."

The Qur'an claims that Jesus *was not* crucified on a cross, but that a story was made up to that effect. Instead, Jesus was taken up by Allah to be with Allah. Remember the inscription (see page 17) on the inside of the Dome of the Rock states: "... Far be it removed from His transcendent majesty that He should have a son. ..."

Likewise, the Shahadatan proclaims, "There is no God but Allah, and Mohammed is his messenger." Mohammed is superior over Jesus, and Jesus was not the Son of God, was never born of a virgin, nor did he die on the cross as a sacrifice for our sins. To say he was any of these things is blasphemy to Islam.

Yet, the Bible, in 1 John 2:22 clearly states: "Who is the liar? It is whoever denies that Jesus is the Christ [the real Messiah]. Such a person is the antichrist—denying the Father and the Son." John continues this thought in 1 John 4:3: "…but every spirit that does not acknowledge Jesus [Messiah in the flesh] is not from God. This is the spirit of the antichrist, which you have heard is coming and even now is already in the world." According to these two verses Islam represents the spirit of the Antichrist since it adamantly denies Jesus is the Son of God.

Islam and the Qur'an deny just about everything in the New Testament (much in the Old Testament too), except the name "Jesus." For instance, the Qur'an prophesies that the messianic Jesus will return at the same time as the Mahdi, but not as the prophesied Messiah of the Bible. Instead, he will return as a *Muslim* prophet of Allah to help the Mahdi convince Jews and Christians that Allah is the true God, not Jehovah. Jesus is named "Isa" in the Qur'an, which states in 43:61, "And [Isa] shall be a Sign [for the coming of] the Hour [of Allah's Judgment]: therefore have no doubt about the (Hour), but follow ye Me: this is a Straight Way."

When Jesus returns Qur'an 4:159 states, "There is not one of the People of the Scripture [Jews and Christians] but will believe in him [Jesus] before his death and on the Day of Resurrection he will be a witness against them." Mufti's Muhammad Shafi and Muhammad Usmani wrote, that the phrase "will believe in him before his death" means that Christians and Jews will "confirm that he is alive and has not died and he is not God or the Son of God but [rather] His [Allah's] slave and Messenger, and Isa [Jesus] will testify against those who had called him Son of God."[143]

Compared to the Bible, everything is backwards in the Qur'an and Islam. The so-called moderate Muslim favored by former CIA director Woolsey, Sheikh Kabbani agrees that Jesus is not the Messiah and instead a servant of Allah:

"Like all prophets, Prophet Jesus came with the divine message of surrender to God Almighty, which is Islam. This verse

[Qur'an 4:159] shows that when Jesus returns he will personally correct the misrepresentations and misinterpretations and will affirm the true message that he brought in his time as a prophet, and that he never claimed to be the Son of God. Furthermore, he will reaffirm in his second coming what he prophesied in his first coming bearing witness to the seal of the Messengers, Prophet Mohammed. In his second coming many non-Muslims will accept Jesus as a servant of Allah Almighty, as a Muslim and a member of the Community of Mohammed."[144]

These diabolical verses in the Qur'an undermine the Biblical reason Jesus returns during the end times. Christians know that Jesus was resurrected and so is alive today. Biblically, he will return during the end times to save his people and destroy Satan. However, the Qur'an twists this so that non-Christians will likely believe the Mahdi when he tells the world that Jesus did not die on the cross. Instead, he was taken up to Allah and now returns in order to convince Christians and Jews that Allah is the one true God.

It gets worse. Muslims are taught that there is a false god called ad-Dajjal who will come to the aid of the Jews just before the Muslims wipe them out during the Last Days. Sheikh Kabbani warns Muslims against being deceived by ad-Dajjal who will have miraculous powers:

"The Prophet was warning us that in the Last-Days there would be someone who would deceive all of humanity. The Dajjal will possess power over this world... He will be able to heal the sick by wiping his hand on them, like Jesus did, but with this deceit the Dajjal will lead people down the path to hell. Thus the Dajjal is the false Messiah, or Anti-Christ. He will pretend to be the Messiah, and deceive people by showing them amazing powers."[145]

The Qur'an specifically, and Islam in general, turn the New Testament and much of the Bible on its head. That should be no surprise. John warned in 2 John 1:7 that: "many deceivers, who do not acknowledge Jesus Christ as coming in the flesh, have gone out into the world. Any such person is the deceiver and the antichrist." Islam is not the first to have the spirit of the Antichrist.

For those Christians who know the Biblical account of the end times, it has always been a mystery how the world could blindly thumb their nose at Christ when he returns and follow a false prophet. If Islam dominates the world at that time (that is exactly what Muslims believe will happen) then Jesus will be the Dajjal and a false prophet will play the role of Jesus. Because of deceit, they will believe their false prophet is the real messiah.

This is called the Great Delusion of 2 Thessalonians 2:11. That is why Jesus in Matthew 24:23-24 gave a stern warning those who would listen: "At that time if anyone says to you, 'Look, here is the Messiah!' or, 'There he is!' do not believe it. For false messiahs and false prophets will appear and perform great signs and wonders to deceive, if possible, even the elect." Deception will reign. This lie or deception will be so strong that even strong Christians will be tempted. Non-Christians, having no knowledge of the warnings, won't have a chance.

In Islam the roles of Antichrist and messiah are reversed in deception. *If* Islam and the Mahdi are in fact the false religion and Antichrist of the End-Times, then the Muslims will have been thoroughly indoctrinated to see Christ as the Dajjal and their Mahdi as the true Messiah. And, deception will be able to convince billions of people who have rejected Christ, claimed to be Christian in name only, or followed other religions. Why? Because the Mahdi claims to be the "Greatest of All Deceivers."

The Greatest of All Deceivers

The Bible and the Qur'an diametrically oppose each other. They cannot both be right. As Walid Shoebat found to his amazement, the Bible's account of history is verifiable and contains hundreds of prophecies that have been literally fulfilled. The Qur'an has none. Nor does it have any documentation that proves the history it supposedly reveals.[146]

There is one similarity between the Qur'an and the Bible that is impossible to ignore. When Jesus was confronting the Pharisees in

John 8, he accused them of being the sons of the devil in verse 44; "You belong to *your father*, the *devil*, and you want to carry out your father's desires. He was a murderer from the beginning, not holding to the truth, for **there is no truth in him. When he lies, he speaks his native language, for he is a liar and the father of lies.**" (Emphasis added)

The Bible repeatedly calls the devil or Satan a liar and deceiver who will be thrown into the lake of burning sulfur at the end (Revelation 20:10). Paul warns in 2 Thessalonians 2:9 that "The coming of the lawless one will be in accordance with how Satan works. He will use all sorts of displays of power through signs and wonders that serve the lie." So, who is this liar?

Qur'an 3:54 actually brags that Allah is Khayrul-Makiren, which literally means "The Greatest of All Deceivers." The full verse says "And they conspired, Allah also conspired, for He is the greatest of all deceivers." Allah repeats this "honorable" title in Qur'an 8, 30:27; 50:13, 42; 10:21; (14, 16); (43, 79); 86,15f; 7,100.[147] The Qur'an exalts Allah as a liar and deceiver; the Bible identifies Satan/the devil as a liar and deceiver. It is likely they both refer to the same entity.

Ironically, the context of Qur'an 3:54 is found in 3:55; "When Allah said to Jesus, I shall cause you to die, then will raise you up to myself..." Again, Allah claims that Jesus was not crucified for our sins, but Allah himself took him [Jesus] to raise him to himself [Allah]. Incredibly, this claim follows the proud claim that Allah is "The Greatest of All Deceivers."

To believe that Jesus did not die for our sins is to believe that there is no forgiveness for sins and no salvation – the greatest lie of all. Yet, most of the world now believes that Jesus is not the Messiah; even most Kaffirs. These non-Christians, even lukewarm Christians

---

[e] A Pharisee is a member of an "honored" Jewish sect that emphasized strict interpretation and observance of the Mosaic Law in both its oral and written form. In their pride, they ignored the intent of God and made up impossible rules and regulations for everyone that they themselves did not even follow. Jesus saw through their hard hearts and called them sons of the devil because they lead people away from the truth.

will be easy targets for this kind of deception if and when the Mahdi comes. 2 Thessalonians 2:9-12 warns of the Great Delusion:

Satan will use this man of sin. He will have Satan's power. He will do strange things and many powerful works that will be false. Those who are lost in sin will be fooled by the things he can do. They are lost in sin because they did not love the truth that would save them. For this reason, God will allow them to follow false teaching so they will believe a lie [in delusion]. They will all be guilty as they stand before God because they wanted to do what was wrong. (NLV)

It should be noted that the "Arabic word 'makara' means to deceive, scheme, hatch up, cook up, or connive. The Arabic Bible in Genesis 3:1 uses the same word for Satan. Jesus warned in Matthew 24:10-11 that, "[10]At that time many will turn away from the faith and will betray and hate each other, [11] and many false prophets will appear and deceive many people." Tragically, many lukewarm Christians will fall for the lie and betray their fellow Christians.

Jesus again warns in Matthew 24:23-24, "[23]At that time if anyone says to you, 'Look, here is the Messiah!' or, 'There he is!' do not believe it. [24] For false messiahs and false prophets will appear and perform great signs and wonders to deceive, if possible, even the elect. [25] See, I have told you ahead of time." If the Mahdi is the Antichrist or false messiah of the Bible, the deception will indeed be very powerful. It will originate with "The Greatest of all Deceivers."

If you, or another Kaffir, mention Islamic lying and deception (taqiyya) to a Muslim, he will insist the Qur'an does not allow lying: "And cover not truth with falsehood, not conceal the truth when ye know what it is." (Qur'an 2:42). However, the Tafsir, an old but still used Qur'an Commentary, explains this verse: "Allah forbade the *Jews* from intentionally distorting the truth with falsehood and from hiding the truth and spreading falsehood..." This is the way that verse is interpreted by Muslims today. So, even as Muslims tell us Kaffirs that this verse prevents them from lying, they are lying because they believe the verse does not apply to them. Again this is perfectly all right under taqiyya. What else would you expect from a believer of the "The Greatest of all Deceivers?"

Walid goes on to specifically name 43 astonishing characteristics and descriptions of the Mahdi, Allah or Islam and the Bible's Antichrist, Satan or end-time events.[148] While the purpose of this book is not to explore prophecy for eschatological purposes (there is room for disagreement), it is foolish to ignore the astonishingly similar characteristics even in a secular sense.

Most of these Islamic prophecies are in the Hadith. Some come from well-respected Imams (including many thought to be "moderates). Moderate Muslims will try to pass this off by saying they don't believe all of the Hadith, especially the 91st Beautiful Name of Allah, Ad-Daar (Darr) which is The "Distresser" or "Afflicter". Ad-Daar describes Allah as creating evil (yes, evil). Once again, however, this is taqiyya.

The Qur'an makes it very clear that everything in the Hadith is the truth from Allah, and if the Muslim doesn't believe it, then he rejects Mohammad *and* Allah; "O you who believe, obey God [Allah] and His *messenger* [Mohammad and the Hadith] and those in authority among you. If you fall into dispute about a matter, refer it back to God and His *messenger* if you believe in God and the Last Day." (Qur'an 4:59) A Muslim who denies the Hadith not only denies Allah's command, but Allah himself.[149]

The average Muslim it caught in a trap that has no wiggle-room. Whatever he or she may believe in their hearts that differs from the Qur'an or Hadith, the punishment for believing them is extreme; possibly even death. That is why very few Muslims verbally condemn terrorism. To do so exposes them to harsh scrutiny, unless, of course, they can show they are doing it under the cover of taqiyya.

To deny Jihad also denies another fundamental name of Allah. The greatest deceiver and afflicter are not the only titles Allah claims for himself. He also claims the title "The God of War."

7 – Jihad and the God of War

"Make war upon such of those to whom the scriptures have been given [Jews and Christians] as believe not in God [Allah] and have forbidden His Apostle [Mohammed], and profess not the professor of truth..."
(Qur'an 9:29)

Hebrews 2:14-15 states: "[14]Since the children have flesh and blood, [Jesus] too shared in their humanity so that by his death he might break the power of him who holds the power of death—that is, the devil— [15] and free those who all their lives were held in slavery by their fear of death." This uplifting passage affirms that Jesus died so that those who receive him as their Lord and Savior will have eternal life. It also identifies the one who holds the power of death – the devil or Satan.

The Destroyer

In the Qur'an one of the 99 "beautiful names" for Allah is Al-Mumeet; "the one who possesses the power of death, causer of death, the slayer, and the taker of life or the destroyer of life."[150] This is almost identical to John's description of Satan in Revelation 9:11: "They [demons] had as king over them the angel of the Abyss, whose name in Hebrew is Abaddon and in Greek is Apollyon (that is, Destroyer)." Likewise, Revelation 13:4 says of Satan and the Antichrist, "Who is like the Beast, and who can make war with him?"

Nearly every description of the beast, Satan or the Antichrist in the Bible fits the spirit of Islam. Daniel 8 and 11 describe the End Time leader:

[23] "In the latter part of their reign, when rebels have become completely wicked, a fierce-looking king, a master of intrigue, will arise. [24] He will become very strong, but not by his own power. He will cause astounding *devastation* and will succeed in whatever he does. He will *destroy those who are mighty, the holy people.* [25] He will *cause deceit to prosper*, and he will *consider himself superior.* Daniel 8:23-25

"[36]The king will do as he pleases. *He will exalt and magnify himself above every god and will say unheard-of things against the God of gods.* He will be successful until the time of wrath is completed, for what has been determined must take place...
[39] He will *attack the mightiest fortresses with the help of a foreign god* and will greatly honor those who acknowledge him." Daniel 11:36 & 39

While it remains to be seen if the Mahdi is the Antichrist (or any of the dark names the Bible ascribes to this evil), he certainly fits all the descriptions of him prophesied in Islamic writings.

As noted in the last chapter, number 91 of Allah's 99 "beautiful" names (the 91st) is Al-Darr, which is the Arabic word for vermin or anything nasty. According to Shoebat and Richardson, "It literally means the causer of harm, the afflicter and creator of all suffering."[151]

In the Bible, Satan is the one who afflicts people with calamity and suffering. His protégé, the Antichrist (often called the beast) is the one who destroys the saints. He sets up what is called the abomination that causes desolation in Daniel 9:27, "He will confirm a covenant with many for one 'seven.' In the middle of the 'seven' he will put an end to sacrifice and offering. And at the temple he will set up an ***abomination that causes desolation***, until the end that is decreed is poured out on him." (Emphasis added) Daniel repeats the description in Daniel 11:31 and 12:11. Jesus reaffirms it in Matthew 24:15 and Mark 13:14.

Almost all Qur'an-believing Muslims believe the coming Mahdi will wage war against the rest of the world and defeat all other religions and political systems. Then he will rule the world by military force. Islamic scholar Al-Sadr extolls, "He [the Mahdi] will appear on the appointed day, and then he will fight against the forces of evil [you and me], lead a world revolution and set up a new world order based on justice, righteousness and virtue...and Islam will be victorious over all the religions."[152] As the Bible prophecies above confirm, he will succeed in this – for a while.

Many Islamic books have been written extoling the Mahdi's glorious victories over the Kaffirs of the world. Walid Shoebat grew up and "was never once taught that Jihad was anything other than one of Islam's most foundational tenants. Jihad was always taught as a war against the entire non-Muslim world. Islam, Allah, and Jihad are inseparable."[153]

Mohammed and the Caliphs that followed him conquered the Mideast at the point of a sword. They first offered peace – if the nation would but accept Islam as their religion. Given the brutal Islamic reputation, most nations/tribes rejected the offer. The refusal was always followed by a relentless and vicious attack that would eventually overwhelm the hapless people.

Salvation and Jihad

One of the reasons the Muslims were so successful was the promise of salvation and entry into paradise if they fought and died with zeal. Most men wanted to die in glorious combat. In effect, they atoned for their own sins by dying in battle. They had no need of a Savior. Allah assures them in Qur'an 3:169: "And never think of those that have been killed in the cause of Allah as dead. Rather, they are alive with their Lord, receiving provision."

Allah's promise of salvation and paradise if they are killed in battle or by strapping on a bomb is undoubtedly the second biggest lie of all (the first is the denial that Jesus is the Messiah and salvation only comes by receiving Jesus). The Islamist believes it totally and unconditionally.

Conversely, the Bible in Ephesians 2:8-9 promises; "[8]For it is by grace you have been saved, through *faith*—and this is not from yourselves, it is the gift of God— [9]not by works, so that no one can boast." Unlike Islam, no one can be *forced* to convert to Christianity at the point of a sword; it has to be a decision by the person. Anything else is a false conversion. However, to stop with salvation by faith is not the full message. Ephesians 2:10 continues, "For we are God's handiwork, created in Christ Jesus to do good works, which God prepared in advance for us to do." A life transformed to do good works should be the result of salvation by Christ. Unfortunately, this verse is often ignored.

True Christianity is not a religion, but a relationship with Christ. The God who created us loves us more deeply than we can possibly grasp. It is relationship with every single person, and intimacy with us that he desires. It is difficult for those who do not have that relationship to understand it. Most people, including many Christians, see the church as a building and Christianity as an organization whereby salvation is accomplished by doing a long list of do's and don'ts. If that were the case, then no person could ever achieve salvation. Romans 3:9-24 says that we *all* fail and none of us deserve salvation by good works. That includes the "holier than thou" Christians.

Jesus paid for our sins on the cross and God's grace was extended so that we can be forgiven. Salvation is by faith in Jesus. It was the sacrifice at the cross of Jesus that renewed the way to the Father. It was always the plan for Jesus to leave the throne of heaven, come to earth as a helpless babe, and fulfill the blood requirement for the sin of ALL mankind, for every man and woman ever born. The only requirement for us is to believe it and receive it as the free gift it is and make Jesus Lord of our life.

Those that try to earn salvation by good works miss out on the relationship that happens when a person repents and truly turns his or her life over to Christ for forgiveness. That doesn't make them better than anyone else, more prosperous or trouble free. However, by following Christ and the life principles he lays down, we can have a more positive and content life, in spite of the inevitable problems and tragedies that come to Christians and non-Christians alike. How? Through the power of the living God of heaven to overcome the power of sin and the tragedies of life.

The choice could not be clearer. Accept Islam at the point of a sword and live in a world of hate and fear, or receive Christ and live in love, forgiveness and the promise of eternal life – without blowing yourself up. That's not so simple for Muslims, however. Islam and hatred are drilled into them from birth until they become automatons. It's hard to break the psychological grip of Islam. Furthermore, accepting Christ could and often does mean a death sentence if you live in an Islamic nation, or Islamic community within a Christian nation. Yet, in spite of the risk, a literal Christian revival is occurring in some Islamic nations like Iran.

Iran Alive Ministries reports that they have documented well over 22,000 conversions to Christianity in the past ten years. They claim that the actual number is much higher.[154] International Antioch Ministries (IAM) estimates over 50,000 Iranian Muslims converted to Christianity in just two years.[155] Writing in the *Daily Caller*, Reza Kahlili reports a former Iranian intelligence officer (name withheld) that in the "city of Shiraz alone, with a population of over one million, there were 30,000 files at the intelligence headquarters on individuals who had converted to Christianity" in spite of the risk.[156]

The ayatollahs are striking back at Iranians who are abandoning Islam for Christianity. These converts cannot worship openly. They are under a death sentence because they have converted from Islam to Christianity. Iranian intelligence agents are ordered to infiltrate Christian home churches, identifying pastors and members, arresting them, and then torturing them to agree to appear on TV confessing criminal activities, or being connected with Israel or America. Often spouses are arrested and are beaten in front of the other arrested spouse until they collaborate.[157]

Christian pastor Saeed Abedini made numerous trips to Iran and was arrested in 2012, accused of establishing and encouraging Christian home churches. He was found guilty and sentenced to eight years in Evin prison for "threatening the national security of Iran through his leadership in Christian house churches."[158] Evin Prison is known as one of the most brutal in Iran. Saeed is not expected to survive his eight-year prison sentence. This is the brutality of Islam.

Mass conversions of Muslims to Christianity is not just occurring in Iran. It is worldwide – wherever Islam is found. *The Muslim Issue* provides abundant documentation that estimates that millions of Muslims convert from Islam to Christianity every year.

Islamic Jihad is passed off as a "struggle" in today's media. It is supposedly only defensive. The only truth in that statement is that most Qur'an-believing Muslims believe they are struggling to take over the world for Allah. But to believe this somewhat innocuous word is somehow the modern understanding of its violent history is to fall into the trap of taqiyya; lying for the faith. Qur'an 9:123-124 commands: "O ye who believe! Fight those of the disbelievers (Kaffirs) who are near to you, and let them find harshness in you, and know that Allah is with those who keep their duty unto Him. Believers! Wage war against such infidels, as are your neighbors, and let them find you rigorous."

According to the Encyclopedia of Islam, "the fight is obligatory even when the unbelievers have not started it."[159] That is especially true of Christians and Jews who are called 'people of the Book:' "Fight those who do not believe in Allah, nor in the latter day, nor do they prohibit what Allah and His Messenger have prohibited, nor follow the religion of truth, out of those who have been given the Book, until they pay the tax in acknowledgment of superiority and they are in a state of subjection." (Qur'an 9:29) Qur'an 2:191 simply states; "Kill the disbelievers wherever you find them." There are many more admonitions to harm or kill Kaffirs.[160]

Jihad, the Bible and the "Mark"

Qur'an 47:4 makes a simple admonition that should send chills up the backs of Biblically literate Christians: "***Strike off the heads*** of the disbelievers, and after making a 'great slaughter among them,' carefully tie up the remaining captives." (Emphasis added) Revelation 20:4 provides this stunning observation:

> "I saw thrones on which were seated those who had been given authority to judge. And I saw the souls of *those who had been beheaded because of their testimony about Jesus and because of the word of God.* They had not worshiped the beast or its image and *had not received its mark on their foreheads or their hands...* (Emphasis added)

Most Americans have never actually witnessed Islamic beheadings, though hundreds of graphic examples are available on the internet of Islamists decapitating their "enemies." The U.S. even supports many of the groups that commonly conduct beheadings, like the Free Syrian Army rebels.

What is the "mark" in Revelation 20:4 referring to? Revelation 13:16-17 provides a chilling warning: The second beast "¹⁶forced all people, great and small, rich and poor, free and slave, to receive a mark on their right hands or *on their foreheads*, ¹⁷so that they could not buy or sell unless they had the mark, which is the name of the beast or the number of its name." (Emphasis added) Again, the purpose of this book is not to get into eschatology, but Walid Shoebat and Joel Richardson note that Muslims wear or use the following symbol "at every demonstration or gathering you see around the world:"[161]

Translation:
There is no God but Allah, and Mohammed is his messenger

Shoebat and Richardson note: "To become a Muslim (literally means submitter), one must confess to the Shahadatan declaration to demonstrate allegiance and servitude to Allah and Mohammed. This submission is always combined with a commitment to fight the world."[162] The symbol is "worn as a sign of submission around the right arm or forehead… Even the part of the Bible that predicted the beast will mark the foreheads is in the Qur'an and the Hadith: Dabat Al-Ard (literally the Beast out of the Earth) is an Islamic version of the account of the 'Beast of the Earth' in Revelation 13:11. But unlike the Bible, in which this beast is evil, the Qur'an gives him a holy mission to revive Islam and mark the foreheads of all true Muslim believers."[163] (Also, Qur'an 27:82)

Interestingly, one of the "marks" found currently on the forehead of devout Muslims is the zebibah. It is a mark caused by extended time spent with the forehead pressed into the ground, or floor in prayer to Allah.

Revelation 13:18 continues the warning about the mark described in verses 16-18; "This calls for wisdom. Let the person who has insight calculate the number of the beast, for it is the number of a man. That number is 666." Walid Shoebat was curious about the number and was stunned when he read the earliest Greek text he could find;

Codex Vaticanus, AD 350. Rather than the number 666 (Chi Xi Stima) as Greek translators had assumed was the correct translation, Walid was able to read it in simple Arabic as the common creed of Islam Bismillah (or Basmalah), which literally means "In the name of Allah."[164] Symbolically they are almost exactly the same:

The Chi symbol represents the crossed swords ⚔ in Arabic, meaning "Islam." The Xi symbol ξ is the vertical symbol for "Allah" which is normally horizontal ﷲ but not always. The same is true for what looks like a shepherds crook. It can be horizontal or vertical, or in some cases, not even there. The Stigma symbol is the symbol for "In the Name Of."

This is just one of hundreds of modern stylized Islamic writings hailing Islam and Allah that can be easily found on the internet and worn on headbands and armbands. Notice the similarity, yet dissimilarity to the characters above.

Is all this a coincidence? Perhaps, but it would be an almost unbelievable coincidence. Shoebat postulates that the scribes, upon seeing what John had written, believing it to be Greek, transcribed the text into the Greek Chi Xi Stigma.

The minor differences between the three images above also could simply be that John wrote down what he saw. And if what he saw was an artist's rendition on a headband or armband, the characters could easily be askew. A simple internet search for images of Islamic headbands will show the myriad of various artistic interpretations of the Bismillah and other Islamic statements.

Once the change was made from Arabic to Greek, it would be easy to translate the Greek word Arithmos to mean "number" rather than its other definition; "multude." Since the Greek alphabet doubles for their numbering system, Chi Xi Stigma can mean the number 666 by ascribing numerical value to the Greek characters. Caution is advised, however. Many try to divine the meaning of 666 counting the numerical value of someone's name to see if it totals to 666. This is numerology and numerology is one method used in divination. Deuteronomy 18:10 strongly warns against using divination: "Let no one be found...who practices divination or sorcery, interprets omens, engages in witchcraft..."

There is another translation for Arithmos besides "number," however. Arithmos can also mean "multitude." Instead of Revelation 13:18 meaning; "This calls for wisdom. Let the person who has insight calculate the number of the beast, for it is the number of a man. That number is 666," it would instead be translated, "Here is wisdom. Let him that hath understanding discern the multitude of the beast, for it is the multitude of man [Mohammed/Antichrist] and his multitude is In the Name of Allah." A stretch? Perhaps. But its clean-cut simplicity makes it the most devastating interpretation of this verse ever put forward. It's something to think about.

Westerners seem to focus on the most difficult to understand sections of Biblical prophecy like Daniel and Revelation. Instead they should focus on the easily understood passages that are in plain language with no imagery or symbolism. There are far more of these passages than of the more esoteric passages. These understandable, no imagery needed, prophecies lay out exactly what Messiah will do and exactly where he will be in the last days.

A time of reckoning will come. Jesus said he will return and he will. Every prophecy that finds Messiah bringing an accounting and fighting the enemies of God on earth in the last days, finds him fighting nations that, at this point in history, are Muslim nations. That could be why he is calling so many Muslims to himself all over the world, giving them a chance to experience his love instead of his wrath.

The Treaty of Hudaibiyah

Most people who read the mainstream media the past seventy years do not realize that the Islamic nations, as well as Hezbollah, Hamas, the Palestine Liberation organization, have broken every peace treaty they have ever signed. Even the Camp David Accords negotiated between Egyptian President Anwar El Sadat and Israeli Prime Minister

Menachem Begin in 1979 is expected to be broken very soon by Egyptian President Mohamed Morsi. There is a good reason for this. It's called the Treaty of Hudaibiyah or Hudna for short.

Hudna means "A hudna [also known as a hudibiyya or khudaibiya] is a tactical cease-fire that allows the Arabs to rebuild their terrorist infrastructure in order to be more effective when the "cease-fire" [or peace treaty] is called off [broken]."[165] The concept goes back to Mohammed's early days when he only had about 1,500 rag-tag followers.

Mohammed originally tried to reach out to the Jews in Mecca (they had a common heritage through Ishmael and Abraham) but was thrown out of Mecca by the tribal Quraysh leaders who strongly opposed Islamic doctrine. He went to Medina where his following grew slowly.

At that time (as now) there were annual pilgrimages by people of other communities to Mecca in order to worship the pagan Ka'ba (the black cube). However, the Quraysh forbade Mohammed and his rag-tag band of Islamists from entering Mecca; even on a pilgrimage.

One night in 628 AD Mohammed had a vision calling Mohammed and his people to make the pilgrimage. But as Mohammed and his followers tried to sneak into Mecca at a place called the spring of Hudaibiyah, they were intercepted by Quraysh troops who refused them entry into Mecca. Mohammed was shamed in front of his followers by the Quraysh. But, the Quraysh made a tragic mistake that has plagued all who opposed Mohammed and Islam to this day. The Quraysh leader and Mohammed signed a ten year peace treaty that neither side would attack the other. The story is muddled as to who actually offered the treaty, but since Mohammed was greatly outnumbered and humiliated, it is likely he was the first to offer the treaty.[166]

The treaty became known as the Treaty of Hudaibiyah. However, in order to save face, Mohammed told the people that Allah did not mean they were to go to Mecca that year, but that they would someday. He also told the people that the treaty was a "great victory" because he *deceived* the Quraysh with the treaty. Every defeat by Muslims since then has been proclaimed a "victory" for the Islamic nation. At that time until today, Mohammed's followers believed the lie. It should be noted taqiyya was the foundation of Islam right from its very start.

Mohammed also said Allah told him that all of the treasures, the women, and the children from the Jewish community of Khaibar (a nearby city) would soon belong to them all! Within weeks of his humiliation by the Quraysh, he successfully attacked the Jewish city Khaibar, followed by successive attacks on numerous other cities and villages. Islamic terrorism was born.

Mohammed took plunder, made slaves out of the men and children and sex slaves of the women. Even today, Shari'a law places the blame for rape of non-Muslims on the woman if the woman does not have "appropriate" covering.[167] That was the justification for brutally gang raping CBS correspondent Laura Logan in Tahrir Square on the night of President Morsi's 2011 election victory. Rape has skyrocketed in Egypt since the Arab Spring began.[168]

As Mohammed plundered city after city, he and his followers became very wealthy. Non-Muslims flocked to Mohammed and converted to Islam to take part in the plundering. The number of Islamic followers exploded. It could have only happened with the freedom allowed by the Treaty of Hudaibiyah. The Quraysh honored the treaty although it was rapidly becoming obvious that Mohammed was becoming stronger than they were. Within two years of signing the treaty, Mohammed's army was 10,000 strong. Mohammed attacked the Quraysh, breaking the treaty, and shattered the Quraysh army. Mohammed was now the undisputed ruler over Mecca as well as Medina.[169]

Mohammed and his successors repeated the process until Islam swept across the Mideast, eventually crushing the Byzantine Empire (the eastern half of the Roman Empire). The Treaty of Hudaibiyah became the slogan used with every cease-fire or peace agreement ever signed by a Muslim group or nation. They openly brag about it – in Arabic, of course. These treaties and accords are always based in taqiyya. With the to-date exception of the Camp David Accords, *every* peace agreement or cease fire has been broken by the Muslims. Yet, history is rewritten to make the Muslims the innocent party while Israel is somehow blamed.

The Great Delusion

In spite of this overwhelming evidence that Islamic nations and groups cannot be trusted, the West continues to negotiate treaties and cease-fires with them. Mychal Massie, former Chairman of Project 21 of the National Center for Public Policy Research, found that: "There are about 400 recognized terrorist groups in the world. Over 90 percent of these are Islamist groups. Over 90 percent of the current world fighting involves Islamist terror movements. The vast majority of world terrorism is religiously motivated by Islam."[170]

Yet, the West, especially the Obama administration and the progressives of both political parties continue to ignore what Islamic leaders, media and history tell us; there will never be peace until Islam dominates the world in a global caliphate. It would seem like we are living in an alternate universe ruled by delusion and wishful thinking. Perhaps that is because we are.

Islamists and Progressive Liberals Linked?

Why do progressive liberals slobber all over Islamists in the U.S. (and Europe) when the Islamic ideology diametrically opposes so many of the long list of liberal progressive absolutes; like women's rights, including abortion rights, gay rights and gun control? Al Gore had no conflict of interest in selling his TV station Current TV to Al Jazeera even though Al Jazeera spins a positive slant on Jihad and terrorism. The sale occurred after Gore refused to sell it to Glenn Beck, a conservative despised by progressives.

Further betraying Gore's duplicity, the purchase was paid for with oil money; something that should have sent Gore fleeing from the sale. It is telling that both environmentalists and Islamists strongly supported the sale to Al Jazeera. Current TV's co-founder, Joel Hyatt stated that part of the reason they chose to sell to Al Jazeera was, "When considering the several suitors who were interested in acquiring Current, it became clear to us that Al Jazeera was founded with the same goals we had for Current."[171] It is a stunning statement with the blatant anti-American bent of the Al Jazeera network.

Plundered, How Progressive Ideology *is Destroying America* graphically shows how progressive ideology is delusional; backed up with hundreds of examples. The ideology is now destroying much of Europe and is well on its way to destroying America.[172]

When comparing progressive ideology of the 1800s with that of today, *nothing* has changed. In progressive ideology everything is based in emotion and there is little to no connection to reality.[173]

The U.S. has built up well over a $16.5 trillion debt and is still adding a trillion dollars a year, yet President Obama says we don't have a spending problem.[174] We have an $80 to $122 trillion (depending on the discount rate used) unfunded liability of our entitlement programs. Yet, Obama said during his 2013 inaugural speech he will not touch Medicare and Medicaid benefits.[175] This is unabridged delusion. Government policy is now based on lies, emotion and political/race/class warfare not unlike those of Islam. Both are irrational.

President Obama also made it clear in his 2013 inaugural address that he will not compromise with the Republican Party (not that he ever did), and is intent on destroying it and the Constitutional Republic that our Founders created. Like all progressives, both Democrats and Republicans, he is convinced he is absolutely right – just like Islamists. Both attack anyone who disagrees with them.

Obama wants to replace our Constitutional Republic with an all-powerful central government based on "social justice" – just like Islam. True, Islam and Shari'a law is a Theocracy, but both impose tyranny. The information in this book strongly suggests that Obama also wants to make Islam a favored religion in America.

Obama has lied about his own Islamic past and about what Islam truly represents. He has lied so much about everything that an entire website, Obamalies.net, has been created that lists many hundreds of verifiable outright lies and misrepresentations made by Obama. It's so bad that he has been labeled the "Liar in Chief" by his more strident critics. What is most shocking, however, is his unending claim that he knows how to fix the economic problems of the U.S. after a stream of abject failures sprinkled with a few anemic successes.

Never in U.S. history has such a failed president been rewarded by reelection to a second term with over 50 percent of the vote. By January 2013, his popularity had risen to 60 percent – just before it was reported the 2012 fourth quarter's Gross Domestic Product *fell* by

0.1 percent.[176] Even so, it still remained high. It is beyond reason. It is irrational.

There are lots of "reasons" for this delusion. Many of them are valid in themselves. But they cannot hide the fact that America is in a state of delusion. Part of this delusion can be explained by nearly a hundred years of progressive education in our public schools. Many otherwise intelligent citizens no longer have the ability to see the deception. They are no longer taught the skills needed for critical thinking. It has been "educated" out of them with still more lies. The author's book *Plundered* spends two chapters on how this was done. It is almost beyond belief.

Saul Alinsky's book Rules for Radicals has become a bible for most, if not all progressive liberals. Obama has said it was one of the most influential books he had ever read, and provided the foundation for Obama's community organizing.[177] Yet, Obama, and seemingly all liberal progressives, are supporting radical Islam. Former CIA officer and intelligence expert Clare Lopez writes:

> America's involvement in the global Jihad against Western civilization – on the other side of the Jihadis – is accelerating. Instead of standing firm as leader of the free world and defender of inalienable human rights, U.S. policy is shifting demonstrably to the defense of those who systematically deny such rights to their own people and seek to suppress them everywhere.[178]

David Kupelian, managing editor of Whistleblower magazine writes, "…It's a testament to modern America's spiritual blindness that we have chosen – twice – a president who champions both" Shari'a Islam and Marxism."[179] Certainly his Islamic background and association with known Marxists explain Obama's syncretistic melding of Islam, Marxism and a hint of Christianity. But what about most, if not all other progressives? Why would they support Islam when it is so totally contrary to their beliefs?

The link, we believe can be found in Saul Alinsky's *Rules for Radicals*. It would not be a stretch to say that most, if not all, progressives have read it until it is dog-eared. It is beyond the scope of this book to do a complete analysis, but a two things leap out.

First, Alinsky justifies almost any type of lying: "The third rule of the ethics of means and ends is that *in war the ends justifies almost any means*."[180] So progressive liberals generally believe they are at war with the historical America, which justifies almost any lying – just like taqiyya in Islam.

More important, however, Alinsky dedicated the book to Lucifer: "To the very first radical known to man who **rebelled** against the establishment and did it so effectively that he at least won his own kingdom—*Lucifer*." Again, the Biblical descriptions of the Antichrist/ beast and Lucifer/Satan that are literally fulfilled in Islam and the Mahdi strongly suggest that *both Islam and progressivism have the same source* – Satan, the Father of all Lies and the Destroyer/ desolator.

Not surprisingly, in addition to Alinsky's "the end-justifies-any-means" method of destabilizing the existing system, he advocates, "The first step in community organization is community *disorganization*. ...All change means disorganization of the old and organization of the new."[181] (Emphasis added) Again, like Islam, progressive ideology calls for destroying the old beliefs so they can usher in their Marxist brand of utopia. Kupelian continues,

"...there's a perfect logic to the 'grand Jihad' uniting these two ungodly forces against the rare and exotic bloom of individual liberty. Both movements are based on rejection of the God of the Bible and of Christianity and Judaism, which comprise the moral foundation of Western Civilization. Both are fixated to an ecstatic vision of a utopia that cannot exist in reality because it defies all the laws of God and man and human nature and common sense."

Whether you believe in the Bible or not, it is impossible to deny that the common denominator between two seemingly opposed ideologies is Satan – the Father of all Lies and Deceit. It is a spiritual war as well as a physical/political one. There is no way America will succeed in returning to reason and reality by only opposing the physical/political evil that is destroying our liberty and prosperity. While that battle must continue, the real battle must first be fought on our knees at the spiritual level.

Citations

[1] Kristie Snyder. Terrorism in America Coming Soon. *Discerning the Times Digest*, Vol. 1(7), August 1999.
http://www.discerningtoday.org/members/Digest/1999Digest/August/Terrorism%20In%20America.htm

[2] ____The World's Muslims: Unity and Diversity. *The Pew Forum on Religion & Public Life*, August 9, 2012. http://www.pewforum.org/Muslim/the-worlds-muslims-unity-and-diversity-3-articles-of-faith.aspx

[3] Nazila Fathi. Wipe Israel 'Off the Map' Iranian Says. *New York Times*, October 27, 2005.
http://www.nytimes.com/2005/10/26/world/africa/26iht-iran.html?_r=2&

[4] Daniel Tovrov. Ahmadinejad United Nations Speech: Full Text Transcript, *International Business Times*, September 22, 2011.
http://www.ibtimes.com/ahmadinejad-united-nations-speech-full-text-transcript-317114

[5] Ibid.

[6] Mahmoud Ahmadinejad. *Personal Memos*, February 10, 2012.
http://www.ahmadinejad.ir/en/

[7] Director General. Implementation of the NPT Safeguards Agreement and Relevant Provisions of Security Council Resolutions in the Islamic Republic of Iran,. United Nations IAEA, GOV/2012/37, August 30, 2012.
http://www.iaea.org/Publications/Documents/Board/2012/gov2012-37.pdf

[8] Michael Oleaga. Ahmadinejad UN General Assembly 2012 Live Transcript, Recap: Iran's President Discusses "New Order"; US, Israel Boycotts Speech. *Latinos Post*, September 26, 2012.
http://www.latinospost.com/articles/4598/20120926/ahmadinejad-un-general-assembly-2012-live-transcript-united-nations-review-recap-video.htm#7xhdtlrjv0XgzTLD.99

[9] Ahmadinejad Denies Holocaust Yet Again. *Huff Post World*, September 19, 2012.
http://www.huffingtonpost.com/2009/09/18/ahmadinejad-denies-holoca_n_291056.html

[10] Gen. Vahidi: Military Strength of the Enemy was Dead. Mashregh News, December 18, 2012.
http://www.mashreghnews.ir/fa/news/155966/%D8%B3%D8%B1%D8%AF%D8%A7%D8%B1-%D9%88%D8%AD%DB%8C%D8%AF%DB%8C-%D8%AA%D9%88%D8%A7%D9%86-%D9%86%D8%B8%D8%A7%D9%85%DB%8C-%D8%AF%D8%B4%D9%85%D9%86-%D8%A8%D9%87-%D8%A8%D9%86%E2%80%8C%D8%A8%D8%B3%D8%AA%E2%80%8C-%D8%B1%D8%B1%D8%B1%D8%B1%D8

[11] Al Alanba,
http://www.alanba.com.kw/absolutenmnew/templates/local2010.aspx?articleid=274106&zoneid=14

[12] David Kirkpatrick. After Long Exile, Sunni Cleric Takes Role in Egypt. *New York Times*, Middle East, February 18, 2011.
http://www.nytimes.com/2011/02/19/world/middleeast/19egypt.html?pagewanted=all&_moc.semityn.www&_r=1&

[13] 2 Million Egyptians in Tahrir Square Many Chant to Jerusalem. *YouTube*, Uploaded February 19, 2012.
http://www.youtube.com/watch?v=eFspeBZnn_s

[14] David Kirkpatrick and Mayy El Sheikh. Citing Deadlock, Egypt's Leader Sezes New Power. *New York Times*, November 23, 2012.

15 http://www.nytimes.com/2012/11/23/world/middleeast/egypts-president-morsi-gives-himself-new-powers.html?_r=0
___Egypt presidential candidate seeks Constitution based on Sharia Law, *The Voice of Russia*, May 13, 2012, http://english.ruvr.ru/2012_05_13/74584752/
16 Frank Gaffney. Muslim Brotherhood in America. A Course in 10 Parts. http://muslimbrotherhoodinamerica.com/the-course/
17 Clare Lopez. Muslims Use "Taqiyya" to Deceive Non-Muslims about Islam. *Radical Islam*, December 14, 2012. http://www.radicalislam.org/content/muslims-use-taqiyya-deceive-non-muslims-about-islam
18 Ayman Al-Zawahiri . Bin Laden Emerged from the Muslim Brotherhood. *Memri TV*, September 27, 2012. http://www.memritv.org/clip/en/3591.htm
19 Steven Myers. To Back Democracy, U.S. Prepares to Cut $1 Billion From Egypt's Debt. *New York Times*, Middle East, September 3, 2012. http://www.nytimes.com/2012/09/04/world/middleeast/us-prepares-economic-aid-to-bolster-democracy-in-egypt.html?pagewanted=2&_r=2&ref=todayspaper&
20 Separation of Religion and State. *Hadiel Islam*, February 5, 2008. http://www.hadielislam.com/arabic/index.php?pg=articles%2Farticle&id=12025
21 Ayman Al-Zawahiri . Bin Laden Emerged from the Muslim Brotherhood. *Memri TV*, September 27, 2012. http://www.memritv.org/clip/en/3591.htm
22 Ibid.
23 Ibid,
24 ___An Explanatory Memorandum On the General Strategic Goal for the Group in North America. #ISE-SW/1B10/0000413, May 22, 1991. http://www.investigativeproject.org/documents/misc/20.pdf
25 Ibid.
26 Ibid.
27 Paul Richter and David Zucchino. U.S. to build Contacts With Egypt's Muslim Brotherhood. *Los Angeles Times*, July 1, 2011. http://articles.latimes.com/2011/jul/01/world/la-fg-us-brotherhood-20110701
28 ___An Explanatory Memorandum On the General Strategic Goal for the Group in North America. #ISE-SW/1B10/0000413, May 22, 1991. http://www.investigativeproject.org/documents/misc/20.pdf
29 Lt. Col. (ret.) Jonathan Halevi. Where is the Muslim Brotherhood Headed? Jerusalem Center for Public Affairs, June 20, 2012. http://jcpa.org/the-muslim-brotherhood-a-moderate-islamic-alternative-to-al-qaeda-or-a-partner-in-global-jihad/
30 Frank Gaffney, Jr. The Muslim Brotherhood: The Enemy in its Own Words. *Canada Free Press*, January 31, 2011. http://www.canadafreepress.com/index.php/article/32761
31 ___13th Session of the Human Rights Council—Adopted Resolutions and Decisions. March 1-26, 2010. http://www2.ohchr.org/english/bodies/hrcouncil/13session/resdec.htm
32 ___Resolution Adopted by the Human Rights Council 13/16. Combating Defamation of Religions. *United Nations Human Rights Council*. April 15, 2010. http://daccess-dds-ny.un.org/doc/UNDOC/GEN/G10/129/21/PDF/G1012921.pdf?OpenElement
33 ___Promoting International Religious Freedom through Multilateral Institutions. HDIM.DEL/0485/12, U.S. Commission on International Religious Freedom, 2011 Annual Report, October 3, 2012. http://www.osce.org/odihr/94876
34 A Common Word Between Us and You. *The ACW Letter, MABDA English Monograph Series No. 20* October 2012. p. 72 of 258 pp. http://rissc.jo/docs/20-acw/20-ACW-5.pdf
35 Ibid p. 147 of 258 pp.. http://rissc.jo/docs/20-acw/20-ACW-5.pdf
36 ___Dome of the Rock, Jerusalem. *Sacred Destinations*. http://www.sacred-destinations.com/israel/jerusalem-dome-of-the-rock
37 Praveen Swami. Mediator in Taliban-U.S. Talks Backed Kashmir Jihad. *The Hindu*, December 29, 2011. http://www.thehindu.com/news/article2755817.ece
38 ___ISNA Convenes Scholars in Mauritania to Discuss Religious Minorities' Rights, July 12, 2012. http://www.isna.net/articles/News/ISNA-Convenes-Scholars-in-Mauritania-to-Discuss-Religious-Minorities-Rights.aspx

[39] Dan Gainor. Media Ignore Obama Attack on 'Those Who Slander the Prophet of Islam.' *Fox News*, September 26, 2012. http://www.foxnews.com/opinion/2012/09/26/media-ignore-obama-attack-on-those-who-slander-prophet-islam/
[40] Alex Pepper. White House, NASA, Defend Comments About NASA Outreach to Muslim World Criticized by Conservatives. *ABC News*, July 6, 2010. http://abcnews.go.com/blogs/politics/2010/07/white-house-nasa-defend-comments-about-nasa-outreach-to-muslim-world-criticized-by-conservatives/
[41] Unclassified Report by Special Accountability Review Board on Benghazi Attack. December 19, 2012. http://www.state.gov/documents/organization/202446.pdf
[42] ____ Prominent Salafi-Jihadi Cleric Issues Fataw Sanctioning Killing of U.S. Ambassadors, Including Chris Stevens. *The Jihad and Terrorism Threat Monitor No. 4963*, Memri TV, September 20, 2012. http://www.memrijttm.org/content/en/report.htm?report=6690
[43] Lt. Col. (ret.) Jonathan Halevi. Where is the Muslim Brotherhood Headed? Jerusalem Center for Public Affairs, June 20, 2012. http://jcpa.org/the-muslim-brotherhood-a-moderate-islamic-alternative-to-al-qaeda-or-a-partner-in-global-jihad/
[44] Eric Lichtblau and Eric Schmitt. Cash Flow to Terrorists Evades U.S. Efforts. *New York Times*, December 5, 2010. http://www.nytimes.com/2010/12/06/world/middleeast/06wikileaks-financing.html?pagewanted=all&_r=2&
[45] Leonard Leo, Chair and Jackie Wolcott, Exec. Director. *U.S. Commission on International Religious Freedom, Annual Report 2012*. March 2012. P 9. http://www.uscirf.gov/images/Annual%20Report%20of%20USCIRF%202012(2).pdf
[46] Ibid, p 113.
[47] Ibid.
[48] Ibid, p 162.
[49] H.R. 2431. International Religious Freedom Act of 1998. http://www.state.gov/documents/organization/2297.pdf
[50] Interview with Ali al-Ahmed. *Frontline, PBS*. November 9, 2001. http://www.pbs.org/wgbh/pages/frontline/shows/saudi/interviews/ahmed.html
[51] Ibid.
[52] Craig Unger. The Great Escape. *The New York Times*, June 1, 2004. http://www.nytimes.com/2004/06/01/opinion/the-great-escape.html
[53] Biography of Walid Shoebat. Former member of Muslim Brotherhood and a Palestinian Jihadist. http://shoebat.com/shoebat-foundation/who-is-walid/
[54] Shoebat, Walid & Barrack, Ben, 9/11: 3000 Americans for Three Saudi Princes; New details about the Troubling Omissions of Saudi Arabia's wealthy from 9/11 Commission Report. Shoebat.com, September 10, 2012. http://www.shoebat.com/wp-content/uploads/2012/09/3000_Americans_for_Three_Saudi_Princes_091012.pdf
[55] Biography of Walid Shoebat. Former member of Muslim Brotherhood and a Palestinian Jihadist. http://shoebat.com/shoebat-foundation/who-is-walid/
[56] Shoebat, Walid & Barrack, Ben, 9/11: 3000 Americans for Three Saudi Princes; New details about the Troubling Omissions of Saudi Arabia's wealthy from 9/11 Commission Report. Shoebat.com, September 10, 2012. http://www.shoebat.com/wp-content/uploads/2012/09/3000_Americans_for_Three_Saudi_Princes_091012.pdf
[57] Ibid, p 2.
[58] Johanna McGeary. Confessions of a Terrorist. *Time Magazine*, August 31, 2010. http://www.time.com/time/magazine/article/0,9171,480226,00.html
[59] Ibid.
[60] Douglas Farah. Saudis Face U.S. Demand on Terrorism. *Washington Post*, November 26, 2002. http://www.washingtonpost.com/ac2/wp-dyn?pagename=article&node=&contentId=A39091-2002Nov25&notFound=true
[61] Shoebat, Walid & Barrack, Ben, 9/11: 3000 Americans for Three Saudi Princes; New details about the Troubling Omissions of Saudi Arabia's wealthy from 9/11 Commission Report. Shoebat.com, September 10, 2012. Pgs 1-2. http://www.shoebat.com/wp-content/uploads/2012/09/3000_Americans_for_Three_Saudi_Princes_091012.pdf

[62] Ibid, pp 5-6.
[63] Nicholas Kristof. Obama: Man of the World. New York Times, March 6, 2007. http://www.nytimes.com/2007/03/06/opinion/06kristof.html?_r=0
[64] Emerson, Steve, A Red Carpet for Radicals at the White House, IPT News, October 21, 2012, http://www.investigativeproject.org/3777/a-red-carpet-for-radicals-at-the-white-house
[65] United States of America vs The Holy Land Foundation, Attachment A, http://www.investigativeproject.org/documents/case_docs/423.pdf#page=5
[66] Hussam Ayloush. The Investigative Project on Terrorism. http://www.investigativeproject.org/documents/misc/709.pdf
[67] Louay Safi. The Investigative Project on Terrorism. http://www.investigativeproject.org/documents/misc/710.pdf
[68] The Investigative Project on Terrorism.
[69] Heredia, Christopher Gay, Muslims battle oppression, SF Chronicle, June, 2001; http://www.sfgate.com/news/article/Gay-Muslims-battle-oppression-Support-network-2906320.php#ixzz2K3Rgr0o2http://www.sfgate.com/news/article/Gay-Muslims-battle-oppression-Support-network-2906320.php
[70] John Guandolo. Underpublicized Threat Deep in the White House. *Whistleblower*, January, 2013. http://www.wnd.com/2011/08/337321/
[71] Farhana Khera. The Investigative Project on Terrorism. http://www.investigativeproject.org/documents/misc/719.pdf
[72] Hisham al-Talib. The Investigative Project on Terrorism. http://www.investigativeproject.org/documents/misc/720.pdf
[73] Imam Talib El-Hajj Abdur Rashid. The Investigative Project on Terrorism. http://www.investigativeproject.org/documents/misc/721.pdf
[74] Israel and U.S. Wage War on Lebanon and Palestine, Fight Back News, July, 2006; http://www.fightbacknews.org/2006/03/hateminterview.htm
[75] Hatem Abudayyeh. The Investigative Project on Terrorism. http://www.investigativeproject.org/documents/misc/722.pdf
[76] The Muslim Brotherhood's "General Strategic Goal" for North America. Discover the Networks, no date. http://www.discoverthenetworks.org/viewSubCategory.asp?id=1235
[77] Walid Shoebat. Proof: Huma Has Ties to Muslim Brotherhood – Countless Documents Surface. Soebat.com http://www.shoebat.com/documents/Huma_Brotherhood_Connections_072412.pdf
[78] Ibid.
[79] Ibid.
[80] Ibid.
[81] Ibid.
[82] Ibid.
[83] Muslimbrotherhoodinamerica.com
[84] Frank Gaffney. The Muslim Brotherhood in America; A Course in 10 Parts. Center for Security Policy, no date. http://muslimbrotherhoodinamerica.com/
[85] Boorstein, M. & Hosh, A., Anwar al-Aulaqi's death reopens wounds for Dar Al-Hijrah mosque in Falls Church, The Washington Post, September, 2011 http://articles.washingtonpost.com/2011-09-30/news/35274090_1_dar-al-hijrah-mosque-leaders-aulaqi
[86] http://muslimbrotherhoodinamerica.com/the-course/
[87] Obama Speech in Cairo full text, http://www.huffingtonpost.com/2009/06/04/obama-speech-in-cairo-vid_n_211215.html
[88] The State Department's Poor Choices of Muslim Outreach Emissaries, IPT News, August, 2010, http://www.investigativeproject.org/2140/the-state-departments-poor-choices-of-muslim
[89] HSBC money laundering report: Key findings, *BBC News*, December 2012, http://www.bbc.co.uk/news/business-18880269
[90] Recommend The Infiltrator: My Secret Life Inside the Dirty Banks Behind Pablo Escobar's Medellín Cartel, by former federal agent, Robert Mazur.
[91] HSBC Exposed U.S. Financial System to Money Laundering, Drug, Terrorist Financing Risks, July, 2012, http://www.hsgac.senate.gov/subcommittees/investigations/media/hsbc-exposed-us-finacial-system-to-money-laundering-drug-terrorist-financing-risks

92 Kaleem, Jaweed, Sharia Law Campaign Begins As Muslim Group Fights Bans, *Huffington Post*, March 2012; http://www.huffingtonpost.com/2012/03/02/sharia-law-explained_n_1292452.html
93 http://www.icna.org/media-gallery/,
94 Madeleine Morgenstern. 'He Yelled Allahu Akbar: Dramatic New Video Features Fort Hod Victims Demanding Shooting be Classified as Terrorism. *The Blaze*, October 19, 2012.
95 Muslimbrotherhoodinamerica.com
96 Obama administration pulls references to Islam from terror training materials, official says, The Daily Caller, October, 2011, http://dailycaller.com/2011/10/21/obama-administration-pulls-references-to-islam-from-terror-training-materials-official-says/#ixzz2K57HotsZhttp://dailycaller.com/2011/10/21/obama-administration-pulls-references-to-islam-from-terror-training-materials-official-says/
97 ACT for America
98 Nick Wing. Michele Bachmann Not Worthy of Intelligence Committee Role, 178,000 Say in Petition to John Boehner. *Huffington Post*, January 14, 2013. http://www.huffingtonpost.com/2013/01/14/michele-bachmann-petition_n_2472682.html
99 Robert Spencer. Vindicated Bachmann Under Attack. FrontPageMag.com, January 15, 2013. http://frontpagemag.com/2013/robert-spencer/michele-bachmann-attacked-and-vindicated/
100 Ahmed Shawki. A Man and 6 of the Brotherhood in the White House! The Investigative Project on Terrorism, December 22, 2012. http://www.investigativeproject.org/3868/a-man-and-6-of-the-brotherhood-in-the-white-house
101 Is Barack Obama Really a Saudi/Muslim "Plant" in the White House? YouTube. Uploaded July 27, 2010. http://www.youtube.com/watch?v=0Jhx_2TqffE
102 Ibid.
103 Clare Lopez. Muslims Use "Taqiyya" to Deceive Non-Muslims about Islam. *Radical Islam*, December 14, 2012. http://www.radicalislam.org/content/muslims-use-taqiyya-deceive-non-muslims-about-islam
104 Mark Landler and Steven Myers. Obama Sees '67 Boarders as Starting Point for peace Deal. *The New York Times*, May 19, 2011. http://www.nytimes.com/2011/05/20/world/middleeast/20speech.html?pagewanted=all&_r=0
105 Taylor Rose. Benghazi Bungle an Attempt to Advance Islam? The Counter Jihad Report, December 7, 2012. http://counterjihadreport.com/tag/clare-lopez/
106 Ibid.
107 Hillary Clinton. Hillary Clinton Playing With Bengazi Truth? *Wall Street Journal*, January 23, 2013. http://live.wsj.com/video/opinion-hillary-who-cares-/5434BD95-6C37-4E01-B6CF-AC8563C00150.html#!5434BD95-6C37-4E01-B6CF-AC8563C00150
108 Aaron Klein. Sources: Slain U.S. Ambassador Recruited Jihadists. Egyptian Officials Say Stevens Worked with Saudis Against Assad. Klein Online, September 24, 2012. http://kleinonline.wnd.com/2012/09/24/sources-slain-u-s-ambassador-recruited-jihadists-egyptian-officials-say-stevens-worked-with-saudis-against-assad/
109 Aaron Klein. Just Lovely: Look Who U.S. is Helping Now. *WorldNetDaily*, May 22, 2012. http://www.wnd.com/2012/05/just-lovely-look-who-u-s-is-helping-now/
110 Aaron Klein. Sources: Slain U.S. Ambassador Recruited Jihadists. Egyptian Officials Say Stevens Worked with Saudis Against Assad. Klein Online, September 24, 2012.
111 Unclassified Report by Special Accountability Review Board on Benghazi Attack. December 19, 2012. http://www.state.gov/documents/organization/202446.pdf
112 John Guandolo. Next CIA Director Covert Muslim, States Former FBI Counter Terrorism Expert. YouTube, February 8, 2013. http://www.youtube.com/watch?v=WnIMiCIslb0
113 Guandolog Associates LLC. http://www.guandoloassociatesllc.com/About_Us.html
114 Mytheos Holt. Rumor Check: Ex-FBI Agent Claims Obama's CIA Nominee is Really a Secret Muslim Recruited by Saudis. *The Blaze*, February 11, 2013.
115 Ibid.
116 Ibid.
117 Top Obama Officials Now Calling Jerusalem "Al-Quds." YouTube, May 19, 2010. http://www.youtube.com/watch?feature=player_embedded&v=4wglrLBqYxQ
118 Kenneth Timmerman. Chuck Hagel: The Darling of Tehran. *The Daily Caller*. http://dailycaller.com/2013/01/28/chuck-hagel-the-darling-of-tehran/

[119] Alana Goodman. Account of 2007 Speech Prompts Letter from Senators to Hagel. *Free Beacon*, February 15, 2013. http://freebeacon.com/account-of-2007-speech-prompts-letter-from-senators-to-hagel/ Also see: 6) The State Department Has Become Adjunct to the Israeli Foreign Minister's Office. Georgeajjan.com, March 3, 2007. http://www.ajjan.com/2007/03/hagel-in-nj-0-delegates-down-78-to-go.html
[120] Clare Lopez. U.S. Policy Defending Sharia, Not American Citizens, Clare M. Lopez Blog Site, December 2, 2012. http://lopez.pundicity.com/12633/us-policy-defending-sharia
[121] Daniel Pipes. Obama's Dueling Beliefs Expose Moral Failings. Washington Times, September 13, 2012. http://www.washingtontimes.com/news/2012/sep/13/obamas-dueling-beliefs-expose-moral-failings/
[122] Obama's Cousin Interview on Al Jazeera Parts 1-3. YouTube. Uploaded on October 11, 2012. http://www.youtube.com/watch?feature=player_embedded&v=BaA4bGUoVZI Part 1, http://www.youtube.com/watch?v=LRfGmWjr3HQ Part 2.
[123] Obamas' Wahhabist Fundraising Empire. Shoebat.com. http://shoebat.com/shoebat-foundation/obamas-wahhabist-fundraising-empire/
[124] Ibid.
[125] Ibid.
[126] Said Obama...Kenyan Businessman Praises Renaissance in the Kingdom. Sauress.com, March 29, 2011. http://www.sauress.com/aljazirah/1103293283
[127] Obamas' Wahhabist Fundraising Empire. Shoebat.com. http://shoebat.com/shoebat-foundation/obamas-wahhabist-fundraising-empire/
[128] Jim Vandehei and Mike Allen. Obama, the Puppet Master. *Politico*, February 18, 2013. http://www.politico.com/story/2013/02/obama-the-puppet-master-87764.html#ixzz2LLdfDjaq
[129] Joel Polaik. Dereliction of Duty: Obama Did Nothing to Save American Lives in Benghazi—and Lied about it. Breitbart.com, February 7, 2013.
[130] Dtovrov, September 22, 2011, Ahmadinejad United Nations Speech: Full Text Transcript, http://www.ibtimes.com/ahmadinejad-united-nations-speech-full-text-transcript-317114
[131] U.S. Condemns Comments by Egypt's Mursi as Islamist Leader. Routers, January 15, 2013. http://www.reuters.com/article/2013/01/15/us-egypt-usa-mursi-idUSBRE90E12D20130115
[132] Turkey's Charismatic Pro-Islamic Leader. BBC News, November 4, 2002. http://news.bbc.co.uk/2/hi/europe/2270642.stm
[133] Yusuf Ali, Abdullah (1987). The Holy Qur'an: Text, Translation, and Commentary. Elmhurst, New York: Tahrike Tarsile Qur'an, Inc..
[134] Walid Shoebat and Joel Richardson. *God's War on Terrorism*. (Top Executive Media, 2008), p. 62.
[135] Ibid, p. 37.
[136] Ibid, p. 52.
[137] Ibid, p. 46
[138] Ibid.
[139] Ibid, p. 51.
[140] Walid Shoebat and Joel Richardson. *God's War on Terrorism*, p. 141.
[141] Tafsir Ibn Kathir; Al-Baquarah. In: Walid Shoebat and Joel Richardson. God's War on Terrorism, p. 141.
[142] Sunan Abi Dawud, Kitaab al-Mahdi, 11: 375, hadith 4265; Mustadrak al-Haakim, 4: 557; "he said: this is a saheeh hadeeth according to the conditions of Muslim, although it was not reported by al-Bukhari and Muslim". See also Sahih al-Jaami, 6736.
[143] Mufti Muhammad Shafi and Mufti Muhammad Rafi Usmani in their book, Sign of the Qiyama [the final judgment] and the Arrival of the Maseeh [the Messiah]. In: Walid Shoebat and Joel Richardson. God's War on Terrorism. p. 59
[144] Kabbani, Shaykh Muhammad Hisham. *The Approach of Armageddon? An Islamic Perspective*. Canada; Supreme Muslim Council of America, 2003, p. 228.
[145] Ibid, p. 223.
[146] Walid Shoebat and Joel Richardson. *God's War on Terrorism*, p. 67.
[147] Ibid, p. 65
[148] Ibid, pp. 55-175
[149] Ibid, p. 53
[150] Ibid, p. 92
[151] Ibid, p. 154

[152] Ayatullah Baqir al-Sadr and Ayatullah Muratda Mutahhari. *The Awaited Savior.* (Karachi, Islamic Seminary Publications), Prologue, pp. 4-5.
[153] Walid Shoebat and Joel Richardson. *God's War on Terrorism*, p. 105
[154] Track Record. Iran Alive Ministries, no date. http://iranaliveministries.org/page.aspx?n=16&p=Our Track Record
[155] Maxine Bignham. Iranian Muslims Embracing Christianity in Record Numbers. IAM, No date. http://web.archive.org/web/20080726171936/http://www.iam-online.net/Press_release_PDFs/IAMTVrelease_FINAL.doc%20%28Read-Only%29.pdf
[156] Reza Hahlili. Iranian Intelligence Agents Target, Arrest Christian Converts. The Daily Caller, May 10, 2012.
[157] Ibid.
[158] Iran Sentences American Pastor Saeed Abedini to 8 Years in Prison. Fox News, January 27, 2013. http://www.foxnews.com/world/2013/01/27/iran-sentences-american-pastor-saeed-abedini-to-8-years-in-prison/
[159] E. Tyan, "Jihad," Encyclopedia of Islam. 2nd Edition (Leiden: Brill, 1965)
[160] See Walid Shoebat and Joel Richardson. *God's War on Terrorism*, pp. 102-104.
[161] Ibid, p. 14
[162] Ibid, p. 376
[163] Ibid, p. 377
[164] Ibid, p. 370
[165] Truces, Arab Style. Omdurman.org. http://www.omdurman.org/hudna.html
[166] Walid Shoebat and Joel Richardson. *God's War on Terrorism*, pp. 118-121
[167] Ibid, pp 111-113.
[168] Raymond Ibrahim. Radical Islam. February 18, 2013. http://www.radicalislam.org/analysis/rape-epidemic-morsis-egypt/#fm
[169] Ibid, p. 120.
[170] Mychal Massie. Peaceful Religion is not spelled I-S-L-A-M. WorldNetDaily, May 5, 2004. http://www.wnd.com/2004/05/24746/
[171] Jeff Bercovici. Current TV Sold to Al Jazeera; $500 Million Deal for Al Gore and Co. Forbes, January 2, 2013. http://www.forbes.com/sites/jeffbercovici/2013/01/02/current-tv-near-sale-to-al-jazeera-likely-500-million-deal-for-al-gore-and-co/
[172] Michael Coffman. *Plundered, How Progressive Ideology is Destroying America.* (EPI: Bangor, ME, 2012). http://www.americaplundered.com/
[173] Ibid. pp. 61-70.
[174] Wall Street Journal Editorial. *Wall Street Journal*, January 15, 2013. http://online.wsj.com/article/SB10001424127887323936804578230050895623268.html
[175] Barack Obama. President Obama's Second Inaugural Address (Transcript). Washington Post, January 21, 2013. http://www.washingtonpost.com/politics/president-obamas-second-inaugural-address-transcript/2013/01/21/f148d234-63d6-11e2-85f5-a8a9228e55e7_story.html
[176] Moran Zhang. US 4Q Falls 0.1%, First Decline Since Q2 2009. International Business Times, January 30, 2013. http://www.ibtimes.com/us-4q-gdp-falls-01-first-decline-q2-2009-1048432
[177] IBD Editorial. Watch Out, Speaker, Obama Still Channeling Saul Alinsky. Investor's Business Daily, November 15, 2012. http://news.investors.com/ibd-editorials/111512-633630-alinsky-trainers-counseled-obama-to-never-compromise.htm?p=full
[178] Clare Lopez. U.S. Policy Defending Sharia, Not American Citizens. RadicalIslam.org, December 2, 2012. http://www.radicalislam.org/analysis/us-policy-defending-sharia-not-american-citizens
[179] David Kupelian. The First Muslim President. *Whistleblower*, January 2013.
[180] Saul Alinsky. Rules for Radicals A Pragmatic Primer for Realistic Radicals. (New York: Vintage Books/Random House, 1971). Pg 29.
[181] Ibid, P. 116

Dr. Coffman is President of Environmental Perspectives Incorporated (epi-us.com) and CEO of Sovereignty International (sovereignty.net) in Bangor Maine. He has had over 40 years of university teaching, research and consulting experience in forestry and environmental sciences and now geopolitics. He was one of four who stopped the ratification of the Convention on Biological Diversity one hour before the Senate cloture vote. The Biodiversity Treaty is one of the major treaties promoted by *Agenda 21*. He produced the acclaimed DVD Global Warming or Global Governance (warmingdvd.com) disproving man-caused global warming—another major theme of *Agenda 21*. Dr. Coffman's newest book, *Plundered, How Progressive Ideology is Destroying America* (AmericaPlundered.com) details how the American people are being indoctrinated and bullied into a very destructive belief system called progressivism in almost the exact manner the radical Islamists are doing it described in this article. His last book, *Rescuing a Broken America* (rescuingamericabook.com) is receiving wide acclaim.

Kate Mathieson has a psychology degree and is a freelance writer and researcher. She has researched Islam for nearly 20 years.

Made in the USA
Lexington, KY
16 June 2014